Count No 'Count

Flashbacks to Faulkner

Ben Wasson

Count No 'Count

Flashbacks to Faulkner

by
Ben Wasson

Introductory Essay by
Carvel Collins

UNIVERSITY PRESS OF MISSISSIPPI
Jackson

Center for the Study of Southern Culture Series

Wasson, Ben.
   Count no 'count.

   (Center for the Study of Southern Culture series)
   Includes index.
      1. Faulkner, William, 1897–1962.   2. Novelists,
American—20th century—Biography.   3. Wasson, Ben.
4. Literary agents—United States—Biography.   I. Title.
II. Series.
PS3511.A86Z98533   1983   813'.52   [B]   82-24810
ISBN 0-87805-162-7

Contents

List of Illustrations

Acknowledgments

The University Press of Mississippi thanks the following publishers and copyright holders for permission to reprint material used in this book: Mrs. Jill Faulkner Summers for the excerpt from *Sartoris*, for the page from *Marionettes*, and for the excerpts from two of her father's speeches. Random House, Inc., for the excerpt from *Sartoris* by William Faulkner, 1929, reprinted in 1956.

The Memphis, Tennessee, *Commercial Appeal* for the extract from a speech by William Faulkner to the Southern Historical Association.

The Greenville, Mississippi, *Delta Democrat-Times* for the extract from a speech by William Faulkner to the Delta Council.

Photographs courtesy of the following:

Frontis: Mary Wilkinson; p. 29: Dean F. Wells; p. 31: Ben Wasson collection; pp. 35 and 38: Archives and Special Collections, University of Mississippi; p. 43: Dean F. Wells; p. 48: Larry Wells, Yoknapatawpha Press; pp. 51, 54, and 57: Archives and Special Collections, University of Mississippi; p. 62: the Brodsky collection; p. 64: Mississippi Department of Archives and History; p. 68: William Faulkner Collection, University of Virginia Library; p. 73: Ben Wasson collection; p. 76: Tulane University Library, gift of Guy C. Lyman, Jr.; p. 78: Archives and Special Collections, University of Mississippi; p. 80: Victoria F. Johnson; p. 87: John Pilkington; pp. 93 and 95: Archives and Special Collections, University of Mississippi; p. 95 (caricatures): The Brodsky collection; p. 99: the William Boozer collection; p. 138: Ben Wasson collection; p. 143: Mississippi Educational Television Network; p. 144: Meta Carpenter; pp. 146 and 150: Ben Wasson collection; p. 153: Dean F. Wells; p. 164: Archives and Special Collections, University of Mississippi; p. 168 (press owners): Bern Keating; (Welty): Ben Wasson collection; p. 176: Ben Wasson collection; p. 182: Bern Keating; p. 185: Archives and Special Collections, University of Mississippi; pp. 192 and 194: Bern Keating; p. 196: Ben Wasson collection; p. 200 (Ben and Meta): the Brodsky collection; (sculpture): Ben Wasson collection (photograph by Stan Burks)

Publisher's Note

The preparation of this book for publication was finished after Ben Wasson's death on May 10, 1982, when he had outlived his friend William Faulkner by nearly twenty years.

Because of his death, copyediting changes which would normally have been submitted to the author for approval or disapproval have had to depend on the best judgment of the publishers. The necessary changes include: eliminating some repetition; correcting a few discrepancies in dates and sequences; occasionally inserting or substituting words necessary for continuity and flow; deleting a few episodes with which Ben Wasson did not have a personal association and which are only unfounded rumors, such as the well-known story about Faulkner's asking his Hollywood employers for permission to work "at home," by which they assumed he meant in California but he meant in Mississippi—only hearsay to Ben Wasson and documentably untrue. The publisher's effort was to keep these copyediting changes minimal.

It is important to stress that Ben Wasson did not intend for readers to assume that his frequent quotations are accurate word-for-word records of what various people said in the reported conversations, some of which took place more than sixty years ago. As one of his remarks in the "Preface" puts it, ". . . I make no pretense at recalling Faulkner's words exactly as he spoke them, but I do say that our conversations—and those we had with others—are substantially factual as reported here."

The final form of the text has been approved by Ben Wasson's sister, Mrs. Mary Wilkinson, with whose kind permission the manuscript is published.

Preface

I have set down, as lucidly as I can, my recollections relating to William Faulkner and myself. My memory serves me well in some areas, but in others, sometimes of most significance, it fails me completely. Particularly, the reader will understand that I make no pretense at recalling Faulkner's words exactly as he spoke them, but I do say that our conversations—and those we had with others—are substantially factual and are faithfully reported here.

Although my memory does slip a cog or so about specific dates, especially those relating to my move to the American Play Company, my facts are accurate. Of the Hollywood days, it is curious to me that I can remember clearly some things Bill said, while I cannot reconstruct others. Regretfully, I have omitted much colorful material dealing with authors and with many literary events of the period.

If my accounts of some of Bill's reactions to certain personalities during his New York visits seem to stress his obnoxious side, let me say here that, although he could be prickly, he was, typically, polite, forthright, and charming to almost everyone he met.

Whatever my errors in exactness in this account, I trust and hope that I have succeeded in creating a truthful portrait of William Faulkner in the days that I knew him.

Ben Wasson
Greenville, Mississippi, 1982

Ben Wasson: A Personal Reminiscence
By Carvel Collins

That Ben Wasson was helpful to William Faulkner in many ways is demonstrated by his memoir of their long friendship, but modesty prevented his stressing some ramifications of their association.

In early years together at the University of Mississippi Wasson's interest in art obviously was a helpful relief for Faulkner when his writing and literary judgment often were considered defective, a University literary society even refusing membership to him, and Wasson. The University annual, *Ole Miss*, for 1920–21, in its presentation of "Senior Law Class" members points out Wasson's concern with art at the end of this caption accompanying his photograph:

> BEN F. WASSON, Jr., LL. B.
> Greenville, Miss.
> *"From grave to gay, from lively to severe."*
> Sigma Alpha Epsilon; Sewanee '18–'19; Red and Blue; Vice-President Orchestra; President "Marionettes," "Mississippian" Staff.
> A lover of the artistic, but not lacking in practicality.

In those early years, as well as much later, the hospitality of Wasson and his family in Greenville was often a refuge for Faulkner from various difficulties and conflicts at home, and Greenville also offered in a small way what New Haven offered in a larger way during his two early visits to Connecticut, the first in 1918: a chance to be among people who considered writing a legitimate occupation.

1

From the start of their friendship Wasson believed Faulkner was talented. But in the twenties, influenced perhaps by the sometimes conservative aesthetic views of his Greenville friend William Alexander Percy, he wrote a few objections to the ways Faulkner was employing that talent. It was not long, however, before he came to strong support of his friend's work.

For Wasson to be willing when first in New York—and not yet a literary agent but making his own attempt at becoming a novelist—to take time to peddle *Flags in the Dust* among the publishers was helpful to Faulkner in ways which turned out to go well beyond placing that manuscript with Harcourt, Brace. For one thing, it led to Wasson's introducing Faulkner to Harrison Smith, who became for a time as useful to Faulkner's being a published novelist as Howard Hawks for years was useful to Faulkner's being able to continue earning in Hollywood the money which, because of the poor financial return from most of his books, was necessary for his survival. In addition, Smith was valuable because Faulkner trusted him and felt free to discuss with him severe personal problems such as those related to his decision to marry, which he presented to Smith in surprising detail.

Though Smith as his publisher did not advance to Faulkner sums so large as he advanced to many other writers, he did give him advances when Faulkner's books seemed unlikely to be profitable. And because of his faith in Faulkner's talent Smith was willing to print manuscripts which another publisher might have rejected as too strange. In later years Smith had pride, as he expressed it to me, that novels by Faulkner which he had published in spite of objections by others had developed a large following, part of the reading public at last having grown up to some of the books.

After Wasson formally became Faulkner's agent, heading the literary department of The American Play Company, he worked hard to sell his friend's fiction, as surviving letters show. He promoted Faulkner's excellent stories enthusiastically and successfully, and in loyalty to his client/friend even flogged with energy and a straight face such a poor story as the one sometimes titled "Love," and tried to remain outwardly undismayed when, for example, Alfred Dashiell of *Scribner's* magazine responded to his enthusiastic promotion by refusing that story, calling it with accuracy a poor thing affected by Hollywood.

Wasson's work as an agent gave a lift of another kind to Faulkner's career. Leland Hayward, who had become the major force in The American Play Company, was a successfully flamboyant salesman and promoter—as his daughter Brooke effectively records in her book *Haywire*. Especially interested in stage and film, Hayward, through Wasson's business association with him, not only sold to Hollywood the first story which Wasson as Faulkner's agent had placed in a magazine but began trying to arrange Faulkner's first contract as a scriptwriter. Though his initial employment in a studio was not a success, as Samuel Marx of the studio and the late Hubert Starr with whom Faulkner spent much time during that first California job both kindly pointed out for me, it did introduce Faulkner to Howard Hawks, who arranged for a second Hollywood stint and, as mentioned above, many of Faulkner's subsequent contracts. Taking time during several years to write scripts presumably prevented Faulkner's writing more novels, but that time was not entirely wasted because his scripts supplied, as many of his published novels did not, money essential for keeping him fed and housed to write some of the novels which he did accomplish—and Ben Wasson started that chain.

Three forces which brought Faulkner's fiction to the attention of American readers were praise in 1930 from the British critic Arnold Bennett, praise the following year of *Sanctuary* from Alexander Woollcott, and praise more than a decade later from French critics and authors such as Camus and Robbe-Grillet. Of those influential responses to Faulkner, Ben Wasson initiated the early two. He introduced Faulkner's fiction to Richard Hughes, as his memoir reports. Hughes liked what he read and introduced it to Arnold Bennett. In those years the American literatti, feeling insecure and provincial, were especially influenced by British critical opinions. Phil Stone, Faulkner's friend and mentor, told me often that he and Faulkner planned to use that situation, deliberately taking Robert Frost's experience as a model, by having Faulkner go to England in 1925 and attempt to establish there a reputation as a poet which would impress critics in the United States. Their plan did not work out quite that way, but Bennett's statement in England that Faulkner wrote "like an angel" and was "the coming man" brought his work favorably to the attention of literate Americans.

The other boost to Faulkner's publicity which Wasson initiated in those early days was steering *Sanctuary* to Woollcott, who promptly featured it in one of his regular, nationally popular radio broadcasts about the arts. Woollcott's program seems to have been a major force in making *Sanctuary* "take off" into large sales. The general assumption then that *Sanctuary* was pornographic—a conception hard to understand today—did distort the response to too much of Faulkner's subsequent work, but the notoriety was for a time useful to him. For one thing, it was helpful, possibly even indispensable, to the success of efforts by Hayward and Wasson to find employment for Faulkner in Hollywood, which, as mentioned twice above, was financially necessary for him, even his one early sales success, *Sanctuary*, having failed to bring him sufficient money because of its publishers' bankruptcy.

Wherever Faulkner was he seemed to need someone whom he could call on for various small services in addition to the help necessary when drinking had made him ill. Phil Stone, besides being helpful in vastly more important ways, often served also in that mundane supportive role when Faulkner was in Oxford. In California Faulkner relied on one writer in addition to the men Wasson mentions in his memoir. In New York Eric Devine saw to some of Faulkner's minor needs as well as helpfully accompanying him on the train home to Oxford after the severe burning of Faulkner's back. At the University of Virginia in the last years of his life, according to James Silver who was his house guest, Faulkner clearly defined that kind of service which seemed so necessary to him by identifying a visitor who had just left the house as "my man Friday, he fetches and carries for me." Faulkner frequently required from some of his editors services ranging from buying pipes or a chronograph and searching for lost articles and arranging for tickets and flowers to taking care of him in illness. Ben Wasson, like Faulkner's other long-time friend Phil Stone, often added to the much larger aspects of his important help to Faulkner the function of providing for the smaller requirements of his sometimes demanding friend. Feeling that Faulkner had great talent, he gave those apparently necessary services with understanding and good grace, and in more places than anyone else: Oxford, Greenville, New York, and Hollywood.

In New York during the thirties Wasson made useful to Faulkner his acquaintance with writers and other artists, as his memoir shows. Though in many ways a loner, as any genius of his general sort presumably has always been, Faulkner notably enjoyed being with certain creative people. One thinks immediately of John Crown, the musician Faulkner spent much time with in California, and of several among the people Wasson introduced him to in New York. Wasson was sufficiently well known there in literary and dramatic circles during the thirties for a caricature of him to appear among those on the curtain of a Sam Berman-Russell Patterson play, *Hold Your Horses*, when it opened on Broadway in 1933. Among the others caricatured on that curtain were four with whom Faulkner enjoyably spent some time because of his friendship with Wasson: Dorothy Parker, Frank Sullivan, Corey Ford, and Marc Connolly. All of them remembered Faulkner—and Ben Wasson—with pleasure when I asked about that period, which Dorothy Parker said she thought of as "those good days." So Wasson helped Faulkner in New York during the thirties to a supportive social life as he had done in Greenville during the twenties near the start of their long friendship.

Occasionally Wasson speculated to me about possible causes for Faulkner's estrangement during his last years and was obviously troubled by it. As he told John Pope of the New Orleans *Times-Picayune*, "It was one of the most grievous things that ever happened to me." The biography of Faulkner authorized by his widow states on its final page that as Faulkner's casket was put in the grave Ben Wasson stood nearby with Mac Reed, Earl Wortham, "and other old friends." That statement was puzzling, but I assumed it was true, having on the day of the funeral attended my daughter's wedding. But after Wasson read that part of the biography he phoned to say, sadly, that when Faulkner was buried he had not gone to Oxford.

The staff of the University Press of Mississippi when commissioning this piece to accompany their publication of Ben Wasson's memoir suggested I make it a personal reminiscence of our long association, centering on the ways Ben fostered my search for information of the sort which might be useful in attempting to get a better understanding of Faulkner's fiction. I am delighted to do so, for the help of several kinds which Ben gave to my wife and me in many visits to Greenville and in scores of letters among us has been indispensable.

He frequently went out of his way to direct and accompany us to sources of important information. He took us to be introduced to Judge Lucy Somerville Howorth, who, as Ben's memoir records, knew Faulkner at the University of Mississippi and joined him and Ben and others in founding the University's dramatic society. She not only supplied then and later significant information but became a friend to my wife and me. At the time of James Meredith's enrollment as the first black student at the University of Mississippi since Reconstruction Ben drove with us to the University to introduce us to Professor and Mrs. James Silver, who became good friends, excellent suppliers of information, and more. Mrs. Silver had known the Faulkner family first through her long friendship with Faulkner's stepdaughter. Jim had worked with Faulkner in concern for civil rights and had induced Faulkner to give an important civil rights speech in Memphis. Having met Sallie Falkner Burns in Portland while teaching summer courses there, Jim urged me to go to Oregon to talk with her. I delayed because of the added expense in an already embarrassingly costly investigation, but Jim insisted it would be worthwhile. When I did spend several days talking with her I was delighted by her having greater knowledge than anyone else then alive about Faulkner's childhood and about particular later periods. After a time, she asked me to come to Oregon again because she had additional information and documents, including an important letter from Faulkner's mother. Later, after the Silvers had moved from the University of Mississippi to the University of Notre Dame, Jim came as a visiting professor where I had been teaching for some years. Puzzled there by a new departmental situation he mentioned it to members of the Notre Dame English Department, who offered a job which I as promptly accepted, becoming in one more way indebted not only to the Silvers but to Ben for initiating a sequence of helpful events.

Two Faulknerizing trips with Ben come to mind here as illustrations of his help because they relate to quite different aspects of Faulkner. The death of his brother Dean in a crash of the Waco cabin plane which Faulkner had supplied was obviously one of the most traumatic of the griefs in his life. Because Dean was an exceptionally skilled pilot the reason for the accident has always been a mystery to those interested in Faulkner. Hearing that J. M. Sowell, a parachute jumper universally called "Navy," had been performing with Dean on the last day of Dean's life, I tried for some time to find him to ask the cause of the crash. Eventually, with the help of several people including a columnist on the Memphis *Commercial Appeal* who helpfully queried his readers, I learned his address. When he kindly said I might call at his home not far from Greenville I told Ben I would be flying down and renting a car and was looking forward to seeing him when I got back to Greenville after the interview. Ben offered to take me to the interview in his car, expressing interest in Dean's death, which Faulkner with great emotion had talked about to him during their drive home together from California in 1937— a monologue which Ben wrote out and helpfully gave to me.

Navy Sowell, by then no longer an exhibition parachute jumper and rider of motorcycles through walls of burning planks, was an expert auto body mechanic, a widower keeping bachelor-hall in a farmhouse, professional tools and auto parts sensibly spread on the living room floor to be got at efficiently. He made us at home in the kitchen, showed us a scrapbook of clippings and posters from the days of The Flying Faulkners, and told us a great deal. When Ben asked why one corner was missing from the scrapbook, Navy said the rats had gnawed it. Hospitably he took a glass jug of corn liquor from under the sink, gave it one vigorous shake, and looked to see whether we were connoisseurs enough to know that the white smoke instantly filling the air space in the jug was the sign of highest quality. Ben, who had known Faulkner chiefly as a writer, was at the first of the visit astonished and wary. But he became increasingly at ease as he enjoyed Navy's skillfully told recollections of flying men and machines in the period when the Faulkner Waco "bought the farm," and learned about aspects of Faulkner's life and personality with which he had never had any connection.

After a few hours when Navy had answered most of the questions we could think of and had sent the cloudy jug from supporting elbow to supporting elbow on a final round, Ben and I got up to leave, Navy insisting I take the scrapbook as a gift because of his pleasure in the chance the long afternoon had given him to talk about the years of the barnstormers. Having obviously enjoyed Ben's increasing interest in what he had been telling us, he finally, at Ben's urging as we stood in the front doorway, gave an explanation, unique and completely convincing, of the crash which killed Faulkner's brother and the three young farmers who had paid for a "hop" to see what their land looked like from the air. But that is another story.

From among several Faulknerizing trips with Ben the other one I want to recall here was to Jackson, Mississippi,

August 13, 1951, for a visit which Ben arranged with Eudora Welty, whose works Faulkner had admired from early in her career and in the mid-forties had strongly urged upon a good writer in California, Henriette Martin.

Miss Welty's other guests that afternoon included Charlotte Capers and Hubert Creekmore. He had already published volumes of poetry such as *Personal Sun* and *The Stone Ants* and a novel, *A Stranger and Afraid*. He was interested in Faulkner and informed about him, his 1926 newspaper review of Faulkner's first novel having been notably perceptive and prophetic. Charlotte Capers is a brilliant writer whose columns in two Jackson newspapers and a magazine were to have for a number of years an enthusiastic following of readers impressed by her hilariously penetrating essays which often are at the same time very moving, as is abundantly displayed by those selected for republication in 1982 as *The Capers Papers*, with a "Foreword" by Eudora Welty.

Unaffected by a special heat wave in which even experienced residents of Jackson were wilting away, it was an afternoon of some of the best conversation I have ever listened to, and Ben contributed his share. Hubert Creekmore was an excellent talker, and Eudora Welty's statement in her "Foreword" that Charlotte Capers "favors the spontaneous, she enjoys the immediate response, the give-and-take of conversation, in which she is a virtuoso" also describes herself. All of them, for a few hours, demonstrated what Eudora Welty has called, again in her "Foreword" to *The Capers Papers*, "that sensitivity to human idiosyncrasy which very often brings about such a satisfactory evening of conversation between friends. (*Southern* conversation, as we know and practice it.)"

Among the features of the afternoon were considerable talk about Faulkner and a string of anecdotes about a writer

of love stories for pulp magazines, one of the anecdotes
involving Faulkner. In the version of it told that day, which
differed slightly from a version told later, the voluminous
producer of short stories of love, after an attempt at the
longer novel form, was unsatisfied with the result and
mailed her manuscript to Faulkner asking for suggestions
which would improve it. Bombarded by such packages,
Faulkner, for survival if nothing more, long had firmly paid
no attention to them. Not receiving a reply the love story
writer eventually telephoned and asked Faulkner whether
he had read her manuscript. When he said that he had not,
she gave him over the phone a full account of her method of
artistic attack. Faulkner patiently listened to it all, and
when she asked his opinion said only, That's not quite the
way I'd do it, honey, but you go right ahead.

With equal courtesy Miss Welty asked, as Ben and I
were preparing to leave, where I was going next on that
interviewing trip. When I told her New Orleans she said
that she too was going there in a day or so. Because air
conditioning was still a rarity she had reserved an air con-
ditioned room in the Hotel Monteleone in order to be able
to finish a story—apparently "The Bride of the Innisfallen"—due soon at *The New Yorker* but impossible to finish
in the excessive heat. While all were expressing admiration
for New Orleans I mentioned that sometimes when work
there had gone well I would take time out to drive for an
afternoon into the interesting amphibious country along
the Mississippi River below the city. Miss Welty said that
her friend Elizabeth Bowen in Ireland, planning a trip to
the United States, wanted to visit that River region and
assumed she could be her guide. She said she had never
been there, and then with considerate hesitation asked
whether, if I made such a drive on this visit to New Orleans, it would be possible for her to go along. I told her, of

course, that I would be delighted, and we made a plan.

A few days later we met at the entrance of the Monteleone, drove south beside the River, and saw some remarkable sights. But that is another story: "No Place for You, My Love," in *The Bride of the Innisfallen and Other Stories*. Eudora Welty, making with her great skill effective use of people and scenes which she obviously observed with impressive ability during that riverside drive, established in the story a remarkably "real" foundation for a presumably intentionally vague fictional plot in which two strangers who meet at Galatoire's, she a small, compact blonde from Toledo, Ohio, and he a harried husband from Syracuse, N. Y., are somewhat attracted to each other. As they drive along the Mississippi below New Orleans that attraction comes to nothing for various causes, including his being both involved with his wife and a dolt and her being emotionally involved elsewhere. Some years later Eudora Welty in an article wrote that she had merged an earlier, unfinished story into her account of the River setting, and in an interview published by *The Paris Review* said, "That story is the one that place did the most for . . . and *was* the story, really."

A sample of the way Ben's early help extended on and on began when he told me at our first meeting that John McClure had been a good friend to Faulkner in New Orleans in the twenties. McClure was very helpful, letting me meet him when he ended his editorial work at the *Times-Picayune* between two and four in the mornings. We would go to one of the bars in the Quarter and talk about Faulkner for an hour or two until he went home to bed. He was a well-read man with special literary concerns which interested Faulkner and, it seems clear, influenced his writing. McClure introduced me to his wife Joyce who had known Faulkner fairly well, having lived before her marriage at 624 Pirates Alley, regularly sharing breakfasts with Faulkner and William Spratling while Faulkner wrote his first novel in a room at that address. She steered me to William C. Odiorne, a former New Orleans and Paris photographer living in retirement in Los Angeles. Though reports by two interviewers have said that Odiorne remembered little about Faulkner, Joyce McClure's vouching for me, after I had met her through Ben's help, caused Odiorne to report a great deal about Faulkner in Paris and to give me prints and the glass plates of the 1925 photographs he had made there of Faulkner and of places he and Faulkner had especially liked to visit during their frequent long walks about the city. Besides giving his oral recollections he turned over to me five neat typescript packets or volumes of his memoirs. His also naming other people to be interviewed about Faulkner kept lengthening that chain which Ben had begun. And Odiorne's directing me to French places which had interested Faulkner in 1925 was useful not only early but more recently when, during the long process of making a PBS documentary about Faulkner, the producer asked me to go with him and the director to help with the filming in France.

William B. Wisdom of New Orleans first directed me to Helen Baird Lyman after he had shown me two hand-lettered booklets, *Mayday* and a sonnet cycle titled *Helen: A Courtship*, which Faulkner had given her about the time he unsuccessfully asked her to marry him. But Ben made my first conversation with her easier by having told me of knowing her in 1918–19 when she attended college dances at Sewanee, where her future husband and Ben were members of the same fraternity. She had kept up her friendship with Faulkner over several years, had visited

the Faulkners in Oxford, and in an effort to get information
for me even phoned Faulkner from Pascagoula. I mention
these matters so I can bring up to the minute this report of
the way Ben's helpfulness keeps on working, for last week,
on the Gulf Coast, I was allowed to read a "new" letter by
Mrs. Lyman and to learn for the first time the date Faulkner had inscribed in 1939 on the title page of the copy he
gave her of his novel *The Wild Palms*, which draws on her
personality for several of the most attractive among the traits
of its central character. Talking again with Helen Baird
Lyman's family has reminded me of something her mother's
sister, Mrs. Edward Martin, told me some time ago
which bears directly on Ben's memoir of Faulkner: One of
Helen's brothers, a youth in 1925 at Pascagoula, had reported to Mrs. Martin his observation that Faulkner in
discussions usually took an opposing, often startling or
shocking, position, obviously only to stir up argument and
interest. I also heard there last week a pleasant anecdote:
When one of Helen Baird's relatives, a very young girl in
1925 at Pascagoula, asked what she and "Bill" did out on
the pier when they were there so long in the summer
nights, Helen replied, "He tells me fairy stories."

Ben's speaking of the time Faulkner and Lillian Hellman
and Dashiell Hammett spent together led me early to ask
mutual friends to introduce me to Miss Hellman. She was a
fine source of information over a number of years of conversations. She once arranged a dinner and evening when her
only guests were Dorothy Parker and I so Mrs. Parker
could talk about her recollections of Faulkner. Later, because of Miss Hellman's considerately arranging that evening on the Vineyard, Dorothy Parker talked with me
again, in California. Lillian Hellman from the start of our
conversations had stressed that I must discuss Faulkner
with Dashiell Hammett when he was released from the

federal penetentiary. A day came when she phoned in pleasant excitement to say, "They've sprung him," and to urge me to come quickly to the Vineyard to talk with Hammett. He then and later had entertaining and significant recollections about Faulkner and in addition suggested other people I might talk with. So, again, link added to link after Ben supplied the first one.

Ben had early spoken of Faulkner's association with Nathanael West in California. Lillian Hellman and Dashiell Hammett had added information about Faulkner's previous contact with West in New York, and she arranged for me to talk with West's sister and her husband, S. J. Perleman, who cut away some nonsense from the frequently published accounts of joint hunting trips by West and Faulkner. It was from Ben I also heard about Stanley Rose, at whose Hollywood Boulevard bookstore Faulkner, West, Hammett, and others spent pleasant time, as Ben's memoir says. Thanks to that early lead it was possible to talk with one of Rose's former long-time employees, who recalled interesting aspects of Rose and Faulkner which so far have not appeared in the volumes published about Faulkner or West. She recalled with pleasure, among other things, the way Faulkner and Meta Wilde seemed to be enjoying each other's company when they browsed through the books at the store. She thought it amusing that the satchels of books Rose took to sell in movie studio offices, which Ben mentions in his memoir, originally carried books on the top and bottles of liquor on the bottom. When prohibition ended, Rose went full-time into books, about which she said he had excellent judgment. His two-room art gallery at the store was ahead of the local time, displaying for sale while Faulkner was often there prints and paintings which she said California then thought extremely advanced. One painting, by a Fauvist, Rose sold for four thousand dollars, which she felt then to be a large sum, in itself and for such a painting.

As time passed Ben often gave me publicity helpful to gathering information or defended me whenever he felt defense was possible. He now and then wrote favorably about my research attempts in his regular arts column for the Greenville *Delta Democrat-Times*. As a result several people said they were willing to be interviewed because of Ben's vouching for me in print.

A master's thesis written by one of Ben's acquaintances had violently objected to my saying in a review of *A Fable* for the New York *Times Book Review* that when writing the novel Faulkner drew in detail on Passion Week and that it was not the first time he had used a parallel to the same characters and events, for he earlier had done so, in reverse but elaborately, in *The Sound and the Fury*. To this then new idea the thesis responded in outrage, saying there was not a shred of evidence to support that absurd view and such criticism must be stamped out. Ben, with a combination of concern and great amusement, arranged a missionary house call which, after an enjoyable evening, seemed to be successful, with the thesis writer born again.

At one point Ben learned from Ella Somerville—his friend from the Marionettes days which he recalls in his memoir—that Faulkner's sister-in-law had convinced her and others, including Faulkner's wife, that Faulkner was angry with me. Her statement was that he had furiously expressed to her his resentment of the way my two-part article in *Life* magazine had treated him. Because I did not write that article, Ben, without my knowledge, supportively convinced Ella Somerville that Faulkner's sister-in-law had confused my name with the name of the author of the article. He also pointed out to her, he told me the next time I was in Greenville, one thing he thought ironical.

Life originally had asked me to write the article and I had agreed but only if Faulkner approved. Through Phil Stone, Faulkner said he did not want *Life* to publish an article about him; so I declined to write it, and the magazine assigned it to a staff member. Faulkner later, at his daughter's wedding, thanked me for agreeing not to write the article and suggested that perhaps I should have written it because, he said with sardonic amusement, "At least you've studied some of my books." Oddly, that misconception by Mrs. Faulkner's sister, though damaging in one way, surprisingly led to significant information because "out of the blue" some people in Oxford asked me to call and when I did, offered recollections and a small number of documents. One of them said, with laughter and to my astonishment, that if I had that opposition I "couldn't be all bad." But the others, more simply, said they were glad that Ben (invaluably helpful as ever) had clarified the matter.

Over the years Ben always found amusing—to him—the log-rolling which came to be more frequent in the Faulkner Industry than in other scholarly efforts to understand American literature. His amusement was helpful by being infectious enough to give a better perspective and reduce some of the irritation at the waste. One aspect of it all seemed to him especially humorous because of his initial involvement with it. He early had advised me not to make several of my better sources freely available to one student of Faulkner. When I naively disregarded that advice and the sources were misappropriated in an especially unfortunate way, Ben's ironical enjoyment of the situation showed me it was funny as well as disappointing. When he later pointed out reviews associated with that student of Faulkner which seemed chiefly to stress my not supplying sources, Ben said, still with intentionally therapeutic amusement, "He's just cross not to have more stuff to lift."

Ben had many useful recollections about Faulkner's reading. One example was his sending me early to contemporary treatments of Saint Francis which were helpful for thinking about how Faulkner wrote *Mayday* and *The Sound and the Fury*. Another was his recollection that when he and his father were discussing a current scandal, Faulkner supplied, from his reading of Havelock Ellis, an explanation of the condition involved and identified it as "lesbian," a term, according to Ben, which neither he nor his father had ever heard before.

Ben volunteered to find current addresses of surviving people whose names I gave him from long lists of friends and acquaintances which Phil Stone and Faulkner had compiled in the mid-twenties for promoting sales of *The Marble Faun*. Many of those people provided useful information, one, for example, having a sad but pertinent memory of seeing Faulkner playing a role on his way home by train from R.A.F. ground school in Toronto.

When mutual acquaintances wanted to raise money quickly by selling Faulkner documents, I sometimes asked Ben to put them in touch with his collector friends, which he did at once out of concern for their need.

In addition to everything else Ben supplied documents. He let me photocopy a play Faulkner had written in college during a period when, Ben joked, Faulkner was such an anglophile "he probably wore tweed underwear." It is not a good play, and Ben, feeling then that it was even worse than he later decided it was, wondered whether it should be preserved, its dialogue being, according to him then, only "Jolly digs you have here, old chap"/"Thank you, old chap," and its chief action, again according to Ben, the men's rubbing tobacco pipes against their noses to polish the briar.

He also let me photocopy an early typescript of *The*

Marble Faun and several poems, some of which Faulkner
included in the typescript booklet *Vision in Spring* which
he gave to Estelle. It has been interesting to make com-
parisons among those *Vision in Spring* poems and Ben's
versions of them and the versions which Faulkner gave to
Katherine Lawless.

About the only difference of opinion Ben and I had
which I can remember concerned two aspects of the plan
for his memoir of Faulkner, which he first told me in July of
1964 he was starting to write. When he finished the first
version he asked me to criticize it. I at once gave him two
suggestions. It seemed to me that he was inviting attack by
presenting as direct quotations lengthy statements made
much too long ago for memory to be so accurate about their
precise wording. When the biography of Faulkner authorized by his widow appeared and that objection was
made against its direct quotation of decades-old conversations, Ben told me he understood the point but repeated
the response he earlier had made: He wanted to give the
effect of immediacy and knew no other way; so he would
warn in his text that though he felt the gist of the conversations was accurate the precise wording was not.

The other point about his plan for the memoir concerned
its title, *Count No 'Count*. That slight shortening of "Count
No Account" was a derogatory name students and some
townspeople applied to Faulkner, presumably because he
wore parts of his uniform for a time after the war, wrote
poetry, seemed quite self-sufficient, and apparently did not
work at anything. The name in its further shortened form
dogged him in his first college year, even the University
annual formally listing him on the "Roll" of the "Freshman
Literary Class" as "Falkner, Count William" and the student newspaper often calling him "Count." The name hung
on even through his postmastership at the University when

he was no longer a student, and alumni from that time would in conversation years later speak of him, without thinking about it, as "the Count." Some who are interested in Faulkner and not aware that the name was derogatory have incorrectly assumed Faulkner himself chose it. One of the best of literary biographers, briefly entering an unfamiliar area of study, wrote about the interest in a romantic past which, his article says, Faulkner shared with Don Quixote. He added that "Faulkner as a young man wore a monocle and called himself 'the Count,' as a simple country gentleman in Spain called himself a don." I suggested to Ben that with so much confusion around it probably was a mistake to emphasize by the title of his memoir the early period when Faulkner bore a disrespectful nickname and that he might want to choose a more neutral title or even one suggestive of Faulkner's later position as the best novelist our country has produced so far in this century. Ben said he of course knew all that but hoped by his title to emphasize that point, a prophet not honored at home later honored around the world. He added, probably correctly, that readers of his memoir would understand.

It was rare that I could do anything for Ben in our long association, which seemed to consist only of his fostering my investigation. But when I drove through Greenville on the way to Oxford at the time Ben, Hodding Carter, and Kenneth Haxton were preparing to publish Faulkner's *Notes on a Horsethief* at their Levee Press, Ben did ask a favor. Several special difficulties had come up during the proofreading of the book, and Ben said that because I was to stay at Faulkner's he wondered whether it would be too much trouble for me to take along those problem passages and ask their author to solve them. Faulkner did it after breakfast the first morning with notable speed, hesitating over nothing. Ben later insisted I accept as reward, for

almost nonexistent service, the final page of the typescript, containing four lines not used in the book and
Faulkner's hand-written request that the book end before
those lines. So I was more rather than less in debt to Ben.

Among the people I met through Ben and profited per-
sonally and professionally from knowing are Bern and
Franke Keating of Greenville. In addition to supplying information about Faulkner, Bern generously gave me the
glass photographic plates on which he had copied the outline of *A Fable* that Faulkner had written on his study wall.
They will be useful in discussing whether Faulkner did or
did not rewrite that outline after painters allegedly covered
the original. For him to put the outline there to guide his
revision of *A Fable* was one thing, but if he rewrote it to
restore an artifact to Rowan Oak as a future "shrine" that
would be something else.

In the Keatings' fine book *Mississippi*, which the University Press published at Jackson in 1982, is an excellent
photograph by Franke of Ben Wasson. Beside him is the
sculptured clay head of Faulkner which often was associated with Ben during his late years. In a September 2,
1963, letter he said it had occurred to him that morning
how good it would be to get the University of Mississippi to
commission the Greenville sculptor Leon Koury to make a
bronze bust of Faulkner for the University Library. His
plan was accomplished and the bronze head has been a
feature of the Library's Mississippi Room. The sculptor, in
gratitude to Ben, gave him the original clay head from
which the bronze was cast. When Ben's sister Mary Wilkinson phoned last May to tell me of Ben's death she added
that he had asked his family to give me the clay sculpture.
After I mentioned the bequest to people from Oxford, the
University staff looked up pertinent records, which clearly
show that the original contractual arrangement included

the clay as well as the bronze. So the clay sculpture, properly, is now at the University. I am pleased by Ben's wanting me to have it, and it is pleasant also to remember how much enjoyment he had from it during the eighteen years it was in his possession. Arranging the commissioning of the bronze head, now widely known as an attractive item in Faulkner's iconography, was Ben's final direct support- ive act for his long-time friend.

Under Franke Keating's *Mississippi* photograph of Ben near the end of his life with the clay head beside him is this caption by Bern: ". . . Ben Wasson, who was godfather to a thousand talents, not the least of which was the state's greatest voice—William Faulkner." By "talents" Bern meant artists. If he were to add a much reduced term which could include someone gathering information in the hope of understanding several novels a little better, his number for those to whom Ben was godfather would have to be revised to a thousand and one.

Vista, California
November, 1982

Oxford

There was, in 1916, an air of intimacy about the campus of the University of Mississippi, known then, as it is today, as Ole Miss.

In those days the campus grounds were confined almost exclusively in a circular form that gave an overall impression of balanced order. There were large trees, mostly oak, bordering on and spreading over the grounds, giving one a feeling that they had been planted a long time before. Around the campus were the usual buildings: dormitories, library, chapel, medical and law schools, and several others. Some were vaguely Greek in architectural intention, especially the red brick Lyceum Building with its tall white-columned porch.

Gordon Hall, also with columns, was the main dormitory for men. A much smaller oblong yellowish brick building, a short distance from the campus, called "the Coop," housed the small number of female students then attending the University. There were other buildings, many of them run down, that had been used for many generations and now have been demolished. The chancellor's residence was near the campus, on a curving road leading to the railroad station. Most of the professors' houses, of white clapboard, all of them two-storied, unpretentious, were on the same road.

Fewer than six hundred students were enrolled at the University, most known to one another, and it was the custom of the time for students to speak to everyone they encountered.

In October of that year I was a sixteen-year-old freshman, who only a few years previously had learned, with consternation, that babies did not come out of physicians' black satchels. I had seldom been on trips extending many miles from Greenville, Mississippi, located on the Mississippi River in the lush cotton country of the Delta.

At the time Ole Miss freshmen were put through a period of hazing—paddlings, clipping of hair to the skull, obliging the lowly beings to wear skull caps made of, if my memory is correct, green felt.

Soon the trees were scarlets and yellows and reddish browns as the fall semester advanced. The lingering blood-thirsty cries of "Freshman, Freshman" no longer brought fear to me as they had when I first heard them. Upper-classmen were tiring of freshman-baiting as they came to realize that the first thrill of terrorism was ended.

Several upperclassmen had become my friends, one among them, to my great pride, a senior. One afternoon in early autumn two months or so after I had matriculated, he and I were walking together on the campus toward the railroad station—or depot, as it was usually called—to watch the arrival of a passenger train and to gaze at travelers to the legendary and glamorous city of New Orleans or Memphis.

As we strolled leisurely along, a young man came walking toward us.

"Here comes 'Count No 'Count,'" my companion said.

"Who?" I asked.

"Wait until we've passed, and I'll tell you about him. I've met him before. Maybe he'll stop and if he does, I'll introduce you to each other."

The man did stop us, and my friend said: "Ben, this is Bill Falkner." (Until 1918 he spelled the family name without the *u*.)

We both acknowledged the introduction, I by extending my right hand for him to clasp, he, ignoring my conventional gesture, by raising his left hand in a sort of salute.

A white handkerchief was tucked in a sleeve of his tweed coat, which seemed curious to me. I thought he looked quite British. His coat had brown leather patches at the elbows, and his baggy trousers were of gray flannel. His brown shoes were highly polished, and his striped tie I later learned was known as a "regimental." He was a bit taller than I and slender. Above his thin lips he wore a smallish moustache that reminded me immediately of Charlie Chaplin's trademark. His nose was aquiline, his eyes dark, piercing, and almond-shaped.

"You two fellows should get along fine," the senior student said. "You both like to read poetry and highbrow books. Don't you?"

Bill Faulkner didn't reply, and I muttered, "Oh."

"You're a poet, aren't you?" my friend said.

"Not John Keats," Bill said in a low, hollow-sounding voice.

He struck a match with his thumbnail, lit a corncob pipe, and took a couple of draws. Then he held up a hand. "Cheerio," he said, and continued his walk to the campus.

"He sure is a nut," my friend said when Bill was out of earshot.

"Is he a college student?" I asked.

"He's not a student and don't, so far's anybody knows, do anything. That's why he's called Count No 'Count, I reckon. Lives off his family in Oxford—mother, father, and some brothers, I hear. Plays poker. Shoots craps. Drinks moonshine whiskey when he can get it. Dabbles in things, they say."

I refrained from asking what he meant by *things*. "What did you say's his name?"

"F-A-L-K-N-E-R's the way they spell it. Yeah, he's a real nut. Hangs around the courthouse, and you can see him sometimes on the square in Oxford, or just sitting by himself on a bench there, doing nothing but looking."

"Here comes the train," I said, hearing the whistle. "Beat you to the depot." And we raced across the wooden bridge to the station platform. A few days later, my special senior friend stopped me on the campus as I was hurrying to a class.

"Saw the Count in town yesterday. You know what he said about you? Man alive!"

"What?"

"Said you look like a young Galahad who's just gotten off a rocking horse. I told you he's a nut."

I took the remark to be complimentary. Meetings with Faulkner during the rest of the year were, insofar as I remember, few and far between.

The war in Europe was far removed from our own placid lives, too distant to have reality. But we heard of the diabolical Huns bayoneting Belgian and French babies and ravishing the helpless, holy nuns in French convents. The students strolled into town to see motion pictures, plus newsreels, dealing silently but graphically with the horrors of the war across the Atlantic Ocean. We sided with the Allies. There were professors at Ole Miss accused of being pro-German, in particular those who taught the Teutonic language and literature. These reputed sympathizers and the hated Huns were the chief targets of scorn and distrust.

On a day following Christmas holidays, I encountered Faulkner at the campus post office, and he was cordial, asking if I had recently read anything new and interesting. I told him I was much too busy with classes to read. I didn't care to expose my ignorance, especially of contemporary literature, but I admitted to him that I had recently written a few poems.

"I reckon you've been too busy grieving about those Belgian babies on the ends of bayonets."

Someone interrupted before I could reply. I wasn't sure whether he was serious or subtly questioning the truth of the German and Prussian atrocity stories.

The United States declared war against Germany on April 6, 1917, and the world as we had known it came to an end on that date. We didn't realize it at the time but the leisurely, graceful, simple, neighborly, unscarred days were ended.

Soon after our declaration of war I encountered Faulkner as he walked alone on the campus, seemingly wrapped up in the burgeoning of spring. He told me he was making plans to apply to one branch or another of military service, preferably as a flyer. Flying was still a novelty and not generally taken seriously. He said he might go to New York City where he knew Stark Young, the critic and author from Oxford who might be of help to him. "Anyhow," he said, "I'll be in a place where I can look things over before deciding."

Shortly afterwards I heard a rumor that he had left Oxford, and there were different rumors as to his whereabouts—not that anyone really cared. But I realized, as I had from the first, that he was a figure of curiosity and considerable speculation, as he would continue to be until his death and afterward.

Military drilling with broomsticks began on the athletic field. Commencement was held as usual in early June. Romances bloomed and faded, and my first college year was over.

In the summer of 1917 my parents decided they wished me to begin my sophomore year at the University of the South at Sewanee, Tennessee. So, in the autumn of that year I enrolled at that beautiful, magic seat of learning and re-

mained there through the Commencement of 1919, with
the exception of two Christmas and summer holidays.

I went back to the University of Mississippi to begin the
autumn of 1919 as a young miscast student of the law
course, which then required two years. In the first week of
my return to Ole Miss, Bill Faulkner and I met again. I told
him I had brought back to college with me a book of poems
he lent me early in the spring of 1917.

"I wondered who had that book. It's one I particularly
cherish," he said. "Only a fool would let anyone borrow a
book. I don't get 'em back very often, but you seem to take
care of them, so I'll let you have some others. There's some
good new stuff being published now. I'll be in touch with
you. Good to see you again," and he raised his hand in his
half-salute and went on his way.

When I was a small boy in Greenville and was asked,
"What are you going to be when you grow up?" I invariably
answered: "A lawyer, like my daddy and my granddaddy
Wasson." My decision to study law was not brought about
by my avid interest in law, but rather by an inability to
decide on any other career. Law offered the easy way out
for me. Faulkner told me I might be making a mistake
since he didn't believe that I had a special penchant for the
legal profession but had habituated myself for so many
years to "practicing with my father." Bill said he didn't
believe I would be a shining example of an attorney-at-law,
though he said the profession held many compensations.
Phil Stone, of whom he had spoken, was practicing law in
Oxford, so Bill was not altogether discouraging.

Diverse and contradictory stories were told about William Faulkner even so long ago as 1919, and many were to
become apocryphal. It was reported that he had received
flight training in Canada with the Royal Air Force, was

William Faulkner, Oxford, 1918

commissioned a lieutenant, and had talked of receiving his "pips," which hitherto I had thought was a chickens' disease. He also was said to have mentioned "pinks" as part of his military uniform, a term also unknown to me.

It seemed likely that the account he told of crashing a training plane was a somewhat colored, romantic version of what actually happened. None of us who listened to his purported experiences believed half of them. We particularly doubted his account of receiving a leg injury that caused him to limp.

"That's the Count for you. Even a war doesn't stop him from telling tall stories," said those who heard him.

Faulkner enrolled at Ole Miss in the autumn of 1919, and we saw each other more frequently. When he became a member of Sigma Alpha Epsilon fraternity, it was an important event in my life and brought us closer together. That fraternal bond I took seriously, but read now what took place.

He and a younger brother, Murry (Jack) who also was a law student, joined at Ole Miss an underground chapter of SAE, of which I had become a clandestine member there in 1916, a membership I later legalized at Sewanee. Several of the Faulkner men were members of this national organization, and I suspect it was largely because of family loyalty that Bill agreed to join.

Lee Russell, when he was a student several years previously, had not been invited to join a fraternity, and, when he became governor of Mississippi, he persuaded the state legislature to outlaw fraternities and any other closed organizations. Nevertheless, a few, SAE among them, did continue surreptitiously.

When attending fraternity meetings in my freshman year and the next year at Sewanee, I considered the ritual, espe-

Sigma Alpha Epsilon, University of Mississippi Chapter, 1919. Ben Wasson, front row, third from left; William Faulkner, pledge, second row, extreme right

cially that of initiation, to be almost holy. Following Bill's initiation at the country home of Jim Stone, a loyal member, Bill asked me to walk back with him to the Faulkner house on the campus, about three miles away. It was a dark night, and the way led through a thick wood of leafless trees. Bill was completely familiar with the terrain. I was filled with awe, imbued by the performance and words of the ritual, the ceremony having left an almost hypnotic effect on me. I said to Bill what a splendid choice the goddess Minerva had been for our patron.

"Don't you think the ritual's beautiful?" I said.

"All that mythological hash?"

"You're joking." I scarcely believed him.

"Can't you tell when Roman gods enter or Greek gods crash the scene?" It's almost uncanny how those exact words remain in my memory when much more important things have long since faded.

"I miss flying," he said, cutting off further discussion of the ritual. "Man, if I were a millionaire, I'd buy myself a private airplane. Wait, Bud, until you fly for the first time. You'll never be happy to stay on the ground again."

I don't believe that the scoffing remarks he had spoken about the initiation were meant to upset or offend me. He merely spoke his personal opinion, as he customarily did. We continued our stroll to the campus through the dark woods, with him leading the way.

In a day or so he came to my room and held up a slim book, then handed it to me. The author was Conrad Aiken. Titled *Turns and Movies*, the book recounted in an unconventional manner moments in the lives of some people in the worlds of music and the stage. He took the book from my hands and persuaded me to go to the campus with him.

He selected a place near one of the ubiquitous Confederate monuments. We sat there together on the grass, and he read the book aloud to me as students passed to and fro, glancing questioningly at us. Bill read without stopping, straight through the contents. What Aiken had set down moved me greatly.

"Oh, God," Bill said as he finished reading, then set the book on the ground beside him. "This man Aiken has everything it takes to make a great poet—a sense of beauty, of sorrow, satire, humor, compassion, detachment in his talent, maybe it's genius with him, to penetrate his subject matter, an original style of expressing himself."

"But," I interrupted, "its form violates poetry as we know and accept it."

"Good," he said. "Good. It's high time writers broke out of the chains of convention that have held them bound for too long. Exactly what Melville did in *Moby Dick* and Conrad in *Heart of Darkness*," he continued, "and Flaubert in *Bovary*. And even, for that matter, old Walt Whitman. They ignored conventional rules and got ignored. But they slept at night with clear consciences for not violating their visions—the mighty visions of the great ones." His voice was filled with passion.

"Shakespeare, too," I ventured.

"And Keats and Milton and Coleridge and so many others. Sure, Shakespeare, but he could write some pretty tawdry stuff."

Tawdry! I thought, indignantly. How could Faulkner speak critically of Shakespeare? Outright heresy, possibly sacrilegious! Again, he was the teacher, I, the pupil. At a loss for words, I said, "Let's go down to the depot and get a Coke." Near the railroad station was another student hangout, The Shack, rude, unkempt, serving soft drinks, cheese and ham sandwiches, and a few other edibles. We did not speak as we went there.

There were nights when he would invite me to go to the family home of Phil Stone, where Bill was apparently welcome at all times. I scarcely knew Stone then, but he was the first person who believed in William Faulkner's talent as an author, especially as a poet, and continually encouraged him to write and write and write. He and Bill also enjoyed tennis games together.

The Stones' house was situated on a hill about a mile and a half northwest of Oxford. Painted white, with columns on the entrance gallery, the two-story house probably had been erected "before the war." The Stone family must have been away when we paid a few nocturnal visits to the house. Bill had a key to the front door and was familiar with the house and at ease in it. He led me to a downstairs library, most of its four sides lined with shelves filled with books, the "classics" in sets: Dickens, Thackeray, and other famous novelists, plus histories and noted biographies. He told me to make myself at home, as he watched me read the book titles, and waved a hand to a brown leather chair where I sat down. He then went to a large cabinet Victrola in a corner.

"Now for the treat I've been promising. I hope it won't influence you to put away your violin." (Since I was six years old I had taken violin lessons and was a member of the Ole Miss orchestra. Now and then Bill would come to my room and, if my roommate was away, ask me to play.)

"All of these are Red Seal records," he said, going to the table that held a stack. "Red Seal" on a disc then gave a certain cachet to phonograph records, a symbol of the good musical taste of the owner.

He then went to the fireplace and lit the paper under the wood already laid, first fastidiously rearranging the kindling. Next, he went to the Victrola and placed a record on the turntable.

"This is maybe my favorite—Beethoven's Fifth." I had never before heard the Fifth Symphony referred to as "the

Phil Stone, 1912

Fifth," but thereafter I said the term as casually and know-
ingly as Bill did.

He placed the needle on the now spinning turntable.
"Hush," he said, as the music began, and he turned off the
electric chandelier, leaving the room with light coming
only from the fireplace, then took a seat in a nearby chair.
Bill liked to stage a scene.

We were caught up in the spell and surge of the great
musical composition, a triumph of a master. When he
changed the record sides, he did not say a word, but when
the symphony came to a close, he finally spoke. "I only
wish they'd play it at my funeral." He shook his head. "But
they won't. They'll probably select something lugubrious
like 'Nearer My God to Thee.'" He chuckled. "I'll play the
final record again." We had several such music sessions
when the Stone family was away, and I came to know and

appreciate music with which I might never have become familiar.

So, it was not only poetry to which he introduced me and steered me to understanding. In addition to music he awakened my interest in newly published fiction—short stories and novels. He was indifferent to history, autobiographies, biographies and scientific works; at least I do not recollect his showing any interest in them.

I doubt that he felt he was acting the role of mentor; it was more a sharing. There wasn't anyone else, other than Phil Stone, who cared deeply for the things like literature that were thought on the campus to be quite far afield, outré, and, probably, effeminate. He had found in me a young malleable person who liked the things he liked. He wasn't, and never became, a gregarious man. But maybe by being with me and talking with me, there wasn't so much loneliness for him.

I will go back for a moment to my freshman year when I wasn't eligible for the Red and Blue dances, which were only for upperclassmen. The long tables and the chairs in the Gordon Hall dining room were removed for such occasions, and the room was decorated in the prevailing fashion of varicolored balloons and bright paper streamers, giving the otherwise dreary place a gala spirit. One night during a dance I was in my room studying for a test to be given the following day. The alluring sounds of a dance orchestra rising to my floor made concentration difficult. It could possibly have been the orchestra of W. C. Handy, now celebrated as father of the blues. Though he had not yet become nationally famous, his was then the most popular orchestra in our part of the country.

My door opened, and Bill came in. Though to my knowledge he did not attend the Gordon Hall dances, "Down with dull care," he said as if quoting. "On such a night as this," he continued in the same mock vein, "there's no place or time for stodgy studies. Listen, man, listen to that band. Hear that saxophone. Revelry is underway. Let's join it."

"You think I'm deaf and can't hear it?"

"No, not deaf, but dumb, sitting up here in your room when we could be down there with the dancers."

"Not eligible."

"As eligible as anyone to watch through a window." He took me by my elbow and got me out of my chair. "Up," he instructed.

It was useless to protest, so I followed him downstairs and outside to a window of the dining room. We were not alone; watchers were at the other windows.

The couples danced in evening clothes—the men with white ties and tails, the girls in their prettiest gowns. But after awhile I became sleepy. "I'm going," I said.

"Fine," Bill said, "if that's what you want to do. I'm staying."

I left him standing there, rapt with the bright scene he viewed through a window.

The drawings of John Held, Jr., were at the height of their popularity, and Held was at the top of his career. He was the national campus favorite. Bill Faulkner not only esteemed but obviously imitated Held's special style in his own drawings of the long-legged youths of both sexes. Of the Held youths, Bill said, "Held's creatures are almost sexless but they're high-spirited." The girls, or flappers, had an apparently innocent boldness, and the men suggested a lack of fleshiness, but at the same time had a mild satyrlike quality, though saturnine, tall, lean, and quite sure of themselves. Held subtly conveyed the feeling that

Drawing by Faulkner, *Ole Miss*, 1920–21

the young women were not as innocent as they appeared to be.

The pen-and-ink drawings Bill accomplished, though imitation, show his own talent. Several of them appeared as illustrations in *Ole Miss*, the University of Mississippi's student yearbook. They were judged by most of the students to be "nutty." As other art students in Greenville schools had done, I had studied with Miss Caroline (Carrie) Stern, a dedicated teacher. I had come to believe that Rosa Bonheur's *The Horse Fair* was undoubtedly the apex in artistic accomplishment, as, also, according to Miss Carrie's belief, was Whistler's *Mother*, whom Faulkner called, "a very touchy old hen, probably."

He obtained several books containing excellent art reproductions. I do not know who lent them to him—Phil Stone perhaps—but at various times he brought them to me, and we studied them together. He derided my own taste, or lack of it, and through the books which he showed me I began to appreciate the titans among artists, Michelangelo and Leonardo da Vinci leading the list.

He greatly admired the contents of *The Yellow Book* (1894–1897), issues of which he had come by in some way or another. Nowadays, this fin de siècle magazine is generally considered to be effete and esoteric and, all in all, "fancy." At the time Bill praised it, it was considered "daring." The contents, especially the drawings by Beardsley, considerably influenced Bill's own drawing.

His mother, Miss Maud, painted in oils, as well as watercolors. I don't know whether she ever had art instruction, but locally she was thought to be talented, and from time to time she painted portraits of various members of the family, including a few of "Billy."

John Faulkner, just younger than Murry and a few years older than the fourth and youngest son, Dean, also painted and was quite proficient.

Miss Maud and her painter sons were said, in Oxford and at the university, to be "gifted" and "artistic." These adjectives might have been used in derision or praise depending on who said them. Bill's "painting pictures" was deemed to be another of his eccentricities. Painting houses or fences, which he did from time to time, was an acceptable task for a man. Painting pictures was odd. Bill wasn't bothered in the least and never would be by what people thought or said about him.

Quite often (and it wasn't difficult) he persuaded me to join him on his painting expeditions away from the university grounds and Oxford. He would take along a pad of white paper, a box of watercolor paint, and brushes, plus a bottle of water. He would move along in his rather long and determined strides until he arrived at a site he liked, then settle down to paint.

He kept his composition simple and direct and painted rapidly with sure strokes. He painted blue sky with clouds, and he fancied trees in any season, though best of all he liked trees in the springtime—pale, soft greens, light blues. He also cared for unplowed fields, sometimes with birds flying above them. His watercolors were not professional, and he realized they weren't. They were pleasant and captured the mood he felt in what he saw.

When he tired of painting, he'd put aside his materials and remove from a jacket side pocket a volume of poetry and read aloud—Keats, Shelley, Yeats, Shakespeare's sonnets, or a Shakespearean play. (*Lear* he favored more than *Hamlet*, and he doted on *A Midsummer Night's Dream*.) After he had read awhile, he would put the book down and begin painting again.

Many times he said to me, always as if it was an entirely fresh idea, "Poetry's the greatest and most perfect of all the creative arts."

He was happy and at home in the woods. I was not, and hikes, I regret to say, never appealed to me as they did to him.

He liked to play golf, but I never learned the game. He invited me only once to accompany him for a nine-hole game, and he made a mild effort to instruct me in the sport. He must have discovered quickly that I had no aptitude for what he more than once called "the Scotsman's game." At any rate, he didn't invite me to play again.

In those two final years at Ole Miss, both Bill and I found that the creative sap was continuous and hotly rising in us, and, for both of us, it took the form of poetry. Not a week passed at that time of our lives that he failed to show me a batch of his new verses.

Faulkner was writing lyrics, influenced chiefly by Verlaine, Rimbaud, Wilde, A. E. Housman, and several of the so-called Imagists. My own, usually written in free verse, then in vogue, were, I now realize, sorry and puerile examples of verse-making. He would read them, make polite comments, and offer suggestions as to how I might improve them. Although I was completely the dilettante and he a serious poet who studied the techniques and forms of poetry, he never criticized my poetry harshly or unkindly. I did not have at any time the wide knowledge of either poetry or fiction that Bill had. He was an insatiable reader.

He showed me a copy of a small book that he praised extravagantly. It was James Joyce's *Chamber Music*, published quite some time before the appearance of *Ulysses*, which later so widened Faulkner's own fictional horizons.

Among other works that had a terrific effect on him was Conrad Aiken's "Punch, the Immortal Liar," which forecast the writing and method of Faulkner's *A Marble Faun*, the long poem to be published a few years later. I accused Bill of being too strongly influenced by Aiken, and I showed him the Aiken verse, along with one of his own.

"You're right," he said, "and a good thing it was that Mr. Aiken never read my plagiarism. Anyhow, you'll have to admit I showed good taste in selecting such a good man to imitate." He tore his page into small pieces and said, with a kind of sly grin, "I still think my own poem had some good things in it that belonged to me."

During the school year everyone eagerly looked forward to the weekly student newspaper *The Mississippian*. In addition to sports, current events, campus news, and jokes, the paper also published poetry and book reviews. Several of Faulkner's shorter poems appeared from time to time in

The Mississippian, as did a few of his reviews. He was
listed as a contributing editor as he also was in the yearbook, *Ole Miss*.

By far the most popular feature of the newspaper was the
regular appearance of "The Hayseed Letters." Purporting
to be letters exchanged between a bumpkin father and his
son at the University, the crude country humor of the cor-
respondence was hilarious. Although supposedly anony-
mous, the column was written by Louis Jiggits and Drane
Lester. Their reports on the sayings and doings of Count
No 'Count in "The Hayseed Letters" titillated readers. Although some who became targets in the letters were irate
and sometimes threatened at least mayhem, if not murder,
on the perpetrators, the satire was meant to be in good-
natured spirit and it amused Bill.

"I reckon I'll survive Jiggits and Lester," he once said
when he laughingly read a reference to himself in the "Letters." Altogether, he considered the column's rustic humor
to be legitimate and fun.

Miss Maud, on the other hand, was not amused. I was at
the Faulkner house one afternoon waiting for Bill, who was
upstairs dressing to go to town with me. Miss Maud had a
copy of *The Mississippian* in her hand. "Why, they just
make me so mad," she said, her face red with indignation,
"poking fun like this at Billy. They only call him Count No
'Count because they're jealous of him and know he's smart-
er than all of them are put together. I'm going to burn this
up. I don't want such trash in my house." She left me, no
doubt to get a match.

Louis Jiggits became a Rhodes Scholar. He and Drane
Lester are both dead now, but, in their own way, for a
while they had a place in the sun at Ole Miss.

One of the best-loved campus characters at Ole Miss was a

Maud Falkner

Negro man called Blind Jim. He seemed quite aged to us, though he possibly was only in his early forties. In addition to being almost constantly visible somewhere on the campus, he had become the unofficial mascot of the football team and maybe also of other athletic teams—track and baseball. At any rate, a superstition existed among us that if he didn't accompany a team to an off-campus game, Ole Miss was doomed to lose it. Born blind, he was generally believed to be able to identify all the students he had ever met merely by hearing their voices. Whether he was so talented, I never confirmed, but he did have an uncanny ability to recognize a voice.

Anyhow, Bill declared Blind Jim to be a fraud, a conniving character, and a nuisance in whom he placed no belief or trust whatsoever. Today, Blind Jim would have been called an Uncle Tom by others of his race. Bill said that Blind Jim's panderings were a disgrace and suggested in no uncertain terms that the college authorities should put a stop to them. He wasn't in the least amused by someone who had become almost a legend in his own time. Jim would walk along the sidewalks, tap-tapping his walking stick against the concrete, hollering and yelling in his strident voice: "My sho-nuff friends gointer help Old Jim with a little something for his pockets." When he heard someone walking toward him, he would stop dead still, blocking the sidewalk. "Speak," he would cry out, "and I tell you who you is." The test usually came out in his favor, and his reputation for miraculous powers would be further enhanced. Calling out your name, he would seem to be looking directly at you through his dark glasses.

One thing Bill Faulkner found obnoxious was a loud voice. If Bill heard the tapping of Blind Jim's cane, he'd hie himself, as fast as he could, to another part of the campus. Blind Jim was easily more popular among the student body than Bill Faulkner, and I think both of them knew it.

Bill's antipathy to loudness was not confined to Blind Jim's. Another was the noise of a raucous student I recall, who at football games never stopped shouting at the top of his voice. He continuously yelled advice to the Ole Miss team and made snide remarks to the visitors. What he yelled at the top of his lungs was either mindless or insulting. At athletic events he was thought to be a source of witticisms, and a majority of the spectators enjoyed his antics.

At a home football game which Bill and I attended together was this student, nicknamed, I honestly recall, "Hoot." We were seated much too close to him to escape his noise. As the game progressed into the second quarter, he grew more shrill. Unable to bear anymore, Bill rose and announced in a voice that could be heard some several feet away: "A jackass isn't the only animal that brays. I don't own but two eardrums and don't intend to sacrifice them for any jackass in a grandstand." He started descending the steps, moving slowly and deliberately until he reached the ground.

"Hoot" also stood up and cupped a hand to his mouth, and called out, looking around all the while: "Well, John Brown my soul, did ya'll hear what ole Count said to me? I reckon his Royal Highness's ears are too delicate for our kind of fun."

He sat down but continued mumbling to himself, and in a few minutes he was on his feet again, his hand cupped to his mouth, shouting to the teams, loud-mouthed and mindless as ever.

A co-ed noted for her modesty and prudery passed Bill and me one afternoon on the campus. She gave the impression of shying away from us as she returned our greeting. When she had gone, he said to me: "You know, she withdraws the skirts of her mind from thoughts of sex as if it's unclean and might contaminate her." To my young ears, that seemed a remarkably astute and original remark.

At a bull session two of our friends told of an overnight excursion to the fleshpots, where they visited, among other places, a house of prostitution well known to much of the student body. Occasional venery was considered necessary to maintain good health, inasmuch as the young ladies with whom we associated socially did not share their bodies in any casual way. A girl who did was considered to be "fast" and unchaste. She could become a social outcast in the community if it were learned, even rumored, that she was sexually lax.

The two voluptuaries describing their adventures of the night before gave details of the skinniness, plumpness, and ardor or lack of ardor of the "girls" with whom they had briefly bedded down. When they had finished their recounting, Bill said, "A man would be a fool to marry a virgin instead of a whore."

"Hey, man, you're crazy thinking anything like that," someone said angrily.

It was a time in our lives when all women—mothers, wives, sweethearts, sisters, and female relatives—were considered sacrosanct, and virginity deemed the precious jewel of womanhood—in particular, Southern womanhood. The others present vociferously agreed with the first dissenter.

"A virgin," Bill said, "would be entirely lacking in sexual experience and skill, which is the main and basic reason why folks get married—to find connubial completeness."

"Shucks, Bill, you're just saying that to be smart," one of the group said, to murmurs of approval from the others.

"All I'm saying is you better think about it before you tie yourself down to one pure woman," Bill insisted.

The following day he repeated to me in The Shack the same opinions and asked what I thought. I suspect I agreed with him since I didn't know how to explain why I didn't. But his words unsettled me.

"Have you ever noticed," he said one Saturday afternoon, "how whenever two very little girls pass each other— probably never having seen each other before—one of them will give the other a baleful look as if to say: 'Oh, yes, I know all about you'?"

"Sure," I said, "and have you noticed how one woman doesn't seem to listen to what another woman's saying to her?" I was pleased with my worldly observation.

"Why should they listen to one another," he said, "since they already know what's going to be said?"

We were walking on University Avenue, the few blocks between the campus and the courthouse square in Oxford. We neared our destination, in the center of which is the beautiful courthouse, later to be made famous by Faulkner's fiction.

As always on an early Saturday afternoon the square was busy, with the country folks come to town, the county seat of Lafayette County, milling about. Teams and saddle horses were tied to hitching posts, mules mixed among them.

The men were dressed in overalls or gallused trousers and freshly laundered shirts, many of them with no necktie but, instead, a gold collar button. Many of the women wore flowered calico or gingham dresses and, many of them, blue or plaid sunbonnets.

Bill always took delight in finding an unoccupied bench near the courthouse. As we sat together that day, he took a pipe from a pocket, a leather pouch from another pocket, lit up with a kitchen match, then leaned back, relaxed, entirely contented, his penetrating dark eyes bright with interest. He felt he was a judge of horses and commented now and then on a horse or a passing team. Or he might speak admiringly of the mules.

On nearby benches former Confederate soldiers were sitting, and Bill knew a few of them. They seemed very, very old.

"You think they're talking about Shiloh or Gettysburg or the siege of Vicksburg? Well, they're probably bragging about how much 'stuff' they got during the war." It was one of the rare times I heard him use a vulgar expression.

"These country folks you see come from around Oxford, from little places you never heard of even. From mighty fine stock they are, pure Anglo-Saxon. It helps keep us homogeneous down here in the South like it keeps folks in

The Square, Oxford, 1930s

New England congruous. I sure's hell hope we can keep it that way. It gives us our blood strength. Rednecks are what you high and mighty Deltans call our country people. Good, God-fearing they are. Sure, there are plenty of mean ones, slick as they make 'em and sharp as cockleburs in a horse trade." He was conversationally wound up, for it was the longest piece of speaking I had heard from him.

"I like to hear them talk about their crops and their animals and their chillun." He got up from the bench. "Come on, I know where we can get some good corn to drink. Hope you brought along some money."

We crossed the street to Buffaloe's Cafe. He held a private conversation with the proprietor. Then they went through a door and he returned quickly with a paper sack containing the moonshine. I paid for it and we left to start drinking.

In my freshman year I never "allowed hard liquor to pass
my lips," as the old saying goes. I had, though, drunk a few
glasses of homemade elderberry blossom wine, lovingly
prepared by a lady neighbor in Greenville.

My father now and then drank a toddy or in a poker
game perhaps had a drink or two. Nor had I been promised
the proverbial gold watch if I didn't touch alcohol until I
was twenty-one. I just wasn't interested.

At Sewanee I drank now and then, but never to the
extent of a spree or a bender. Good "mountain dew" was
readily available from mountain moonshiners.

When I returned to Ole Miss to study law, I soon joined
others in half-hearted drinking bouts. Bill Faulkner was
considered an experienced drinker who held his liquor well
and also knew where and when to obtain corn liquor from
friends among the 'shiners. He claimed that the leg injury
he had incurred during the war hurt him a great deal from
time to time and that drinking whiskey assuaged and al-
leviated the pain brought about by the injury.

He was quietly sociable when drinking. He talked as the
rest of us did, mostly about women, liquor, hunting,
fishing, automobiles, and God, in about that order. In conversation he was never blasphemous or obscene, and he
did not relate stories or anecdotes about sex or boast of his
amatory adventures or prowess. Nor was he ever obstreperous. He maintained that anyone who could not hold
liquor properly shouldn't drink. He wasn't afflicted with
hangovers and didn't call for a drink, or pick-me-up, on
mornings following drinking sessions. In short, in those
college years he was neither an excessive drinker nor a
regular one.

Until 1920 there was no drama club at Ole Miss. Perhaps at
some time in the past there had been some such organiza-

tion, but I didn't know of it. There was, however, a quite active literary club called The Scribblers, the university branch of a national Greek-letter literary fraternity. To be invited to become a member was considered a high honor, since the membership included not only "serious" student readers of literature, but also several faculty members. Neither Faulkner nor I was ever asked to join The Scribblers, but the omission did not bother us. Grapevine gossip had it that we were blackballed because our literary tastes were much too radical and wild-eyed.

Theater I greatly enjoyed, having acquired quite early a taste for it from my violin teacher in Greenville, Dr. Paul Boensch, who played in the Grand Opera House orchestra, and "passed me through" to a box seat, where theater glamour won my heart forever. I first discussed the lack of a drama club with Lucy Somerville, a Greenvillian and first-year law student at Ole Miss, and I also talked with Bill. We decided, trailblazers that we thought we were, "to do something about it."

A list of prospective members was made from among our associates and friends, and they were invited to attend a meeting in the hopes of starting an organization. Miss Ella Somerville, a member of a prominent Oxford family, whose father had been a law instructor, suggested that we meet at her house. Miss Ella, as we called her, though she was only five or six years older than any of us, and her sister Nina evinced interest in forming the club inasmuch as they took part, from time to time, in various student activities.

At the first meeting which ignored all rules of order, I was elected president, and Bill, on the board of directors, was appointed property man. I suggested that the name of the group should be The Marionettes, and the idea was adopted.

In the *Ole Miss* yearbook for the year 1921, my final

The Marionettes, Ole Miss, 1921

year, there are two full pages devoted to The Marionettes, with a list of members and the board of directors. In the yearbook, also, is an erroneous statement that we organized in September, 1920, rather than in 1921. In addition to those students who were original members, a few faculty members were included, plus two or three non-university ladies who resided in Oxford and who had declared that they wanted to "help out."

Bill drew the pen and ink sketches to illustrate the entry about The Marionettes. These display his artistic skill and the influence of Beardsley, both in the long-legged figures and the marionettes, being manipulated on strings.

We presented three plays. The first two were performed in Robert Williams's motion picture theater in Oxford, and the third in Fulton Chapel, on campus. The audiences' response was splendid. Our final play that season was done at Bill's suggestion, George Bernard Shaw's *Candida*. The members felt it was a triumphant season and that the selection of *Candida* was a brilliant one.

As property man, Bill functioned loyally for the three plays, and he was always more than competent and strictly professional and serious about whatever tasks he did for the productions. From time to time he patiently obtained stage and hand properties called for by the scripts. In many instances their acquisition must have been difficult. I expect we were dilatory about returning the props we borrowed, for we soon established for ourselves a reputation of being not altogether reliable.

Bill also helped with scenery, such as it was. He sawed, nailed, hammered, and offered suggestions for decorating the set and for being correct with costumes. He felt that scenery should "suggest" and not be over-realistic, which was then a novel way of making scenery.

Lucy Somerville directed twice, and Bill was always on hand during rehearsals to help, but he would never act in the plays. "I'll paint, hammer and nail, and do anything else you need me to do, but I'll be doggoned if anybody is going to drag me onto a stage. No, thank you."

He was marvelous for *Candida* and even made posters, which he himself placed in several prominent spots on the campus and in the store windows of Oxford. *Candida* was considered by our sparse audience to be too intellectual, too highbrow. We shrugged off the criticism, believing the carpers to be "hoi polloi."

Now and then during the informal meetings of the board of directors and following a business session, excerpts from plays would be read aloud by one or another of the members, followed by a discussion. Bill elected to read passages from one of the Greek tragedies, in which there was reference to incest. He commented that incest was not the horrible, hideous crime it was thought to be.

There were cries of protest from the members. One said that she did not consider it a fit subject to be talked about at a meeting, especially where both sexes attended.

"Animals are incestuous," he said.

"Shame on you, Bill. You can't compare human beings and animals," an outraged member shouted.

"More's the pity," Bill said. "But you'll have to admit it's lots better to have sex with a sister or a brother, a mother or a father, than with a complete stranger." This is a good instance of his loving to scandalize. The meeting broke up in disorder, and several board members departed in what Bill afterwards called "high dudgeon." The momentary rift he had brought about was soon repaired, and we continued to function smoothly. We had high hopes for The Marionettes, but the organization did not survive many years after we left.

It was about this time in the spring of 1921 that Faulkner told me he was writing a book, printing, illustrating and binding it himself. He worked on it in his turret bedroom, and from time to time he would bring the pages he finished for me to look at. I was almost as enthusiastic as he was, and I complimented him. The title he had selected was *Marionettes* and he showed me excerpts from it.

He bound it in heavy cardboard. It was illustrated with pen-and-ink drawings in the Beardsley style. The hand-lettered text was exquisite and meticulous, and Bill's backward S's, a customary trait in his penmanship, lent the work an oddly interesting appearance.

"Why don't you try to sell it for me to someone?" he said.

"How much?"

"You reckon five dollars is too much to ask?"

"I believe I could get it," I said.

"If you sell it, I can make some more books if you'll sell them. I need money right now. Bad."

I sold the first copy, and later four more to some of our friends. He rewarded me by presenting me with a complimentary copy. It was the first time I had acted as his literary agent. I regret that some years later in New York I had to sell my book to pay medical and hospital bills.

The story, or plot, of Bill's little book was thin, but filled with some truly enchanting poetic passages, though again

are he stops against the sky; perhaps his

heart also misgives him. He stops half turned

toward her and for a fleeting second, he is

the utter master of his soul; tall and the

gods stand aloof watching him, his destiny

waits wordless at his side. Will he turn

back where she awaits him in her rose

bower, or will he go on? He goes on, his

eyes ever before him, looking into the implac-

able future. Perhaps a newer, stronger love

has called him away, that he does not re-

turn; perhaps he is fallen upon by

Two pages from *Marionettes*, Faulkner's one-act play

they showed the strong influence of other poets, Rimbaud
and Wilde in particular, the Wilde quality being especially
evident. Bill owned a copy of the Wilde play, *Salome*,
illustrated by Beardsley.

I have not read the *Marionettes* for a great number of
years. I doubt, however, that anything he ever wrote or
published afterward gave either him or me deeper satisfaction. It was his first book.

The Ole Miss buildings are not noted for architectural
splendor. More than once Faulkner pointed out to me the
"bastard qualities" of the buildings and said that the Lyceum Building was the best on the campus, "with purity
and serenity" it stood, so he declared, with its good, overall
Greek quality. "I'm kind of tired, though," he added, "of
folks describing the Lyceum columns as 'soaring.' You'd
think the columns are getting ready to fly away. My God,

fellow, how I'd love to go to Greece. All that we learned that's good comes from there, don't it?"

The Lyceum, in addition to the downstairs which was used by the university for business and administrative purposes, comprised on its second story and in the right wing a suite of three rooms—two bedrooms and a larger sitting room. Upperclassmen had lived in that suite for several years. Six of us, all SAEs, decided to lease the suite for the 1920–1921 semesters, my final term. With not too much regret, we departed from Gordon Hall, but we continued to take our meals there. Some furniture left by the former tenants gave us a nucleus for our immediate needs in the Lyceum, and after scrounging around here and there, we brought in enough additional pieces to furnish the suite.

Bill said that he hoped we wouldn't put pennants on the walls or pictures of bulldogs smoking meerschaum pipes. We didn't, not because of his wishes, but because we had no pennants or pictures of any kind. Anyhow we were proud of it and thought it was fine enough as it was.

Our rooms in the Lyceum were not ideal for serious studying; they became too popular for idlers, crap games, poker, talk fests, and drinking. Outside our sitting room was a washroom and in the basement were showers. All our attractions, hygienic and social, were conducive to many casual visitors.

Bill sat in on many of the poker sessions. He was a canny player, and his expressionlessness might well have served as the model for the original "poker face." He also displayed skill as a crap shooter, and he could talk in a persuasive, not too excited voice to a pair of dice, speaking softly and eloquently to them as he made his throws. And he never mooched booze. He brought his own with him and shared it.

Poetry was hotly springing for Bill Faulkner in that time

of our youth. Scarcely a week went by that he didn't bring new verses he had finished, or on which he was working. It was in those Lyceum rooms that I read so many of his poems. A few years ago when I paid a visit to the campus and passed by the Lyceum, I was filled with a piercing nostalgia.

The Lyceum building, many years later, was the principal scene of the bloodiest and most shameful event that ever took place on the Ole Miss campus. It was the building where the first black attempted to enroll at the institution. The story of James Meredith is well known. When Governor Ross Barnett took his stand that no integration would occur, federal troops were called to bring law and order to the campus and ensure Meredith's enrollment. William Faulkner had died only a short time before this tragedy.

The campus supply store/post office building was a common meeting place for students and professors at mail-distribution time and a place for date-making, flirting, purchasing soft drinks and stationery, pens, ink, and so forth. The post office section was in the right half of the building. The price of a stamp for a letter in those days was two cents. Through some politicking by his father and much wire-pulling by influential friends, Bill was appointed to the postmastership of the University of Mississippi. It was not, by the wildest stretch of anybody's imagination, an ideal selection. In fact, it turned out disastrously, though, looking back, it is amusing.

The new postmaster was not conscientious in carrying out the duties of his job, nor was he interested in becoming the perfect public servant. In fact, from the outset, he was not interested in the regimen called for. He took no pleasure whatsoever in even half-heartedly performing his

University of Mississippi Post Office, 1920s

duties. He did like to take outgoing and incoming mail bags in a wheelbarrow to and from the railroad station. Now and then, I or other honored friends would accompany him on this cross-campus jaunt, taking turns pushing the wheelbarrow. Murry, Bill's brother, also was employed at the post office, and he frequently went along.

Before long Bill began more and more to neglect his duties. The job wasn't—for any other person—all that boring, but it was too confining for him. The office was cramped. He was obliged to sort the letters and distribute them in the rented boxes, as well as raise the wooden slide of the window to pass out mail, hand out general delivery material, and sell stamps.

His friends hung out there in the work area, and he read or wrote poetry during working hours. As boredom set in for the postmaster, mailbags of undistributed letters and packages began to pile up. Soon, he refused to open the delivery window.

Everyone except the postmaster was in a rage. Bill remained unperturbed and went his own way, reading and writing. It has been said that a few friends formed a Post Office Club with mysterious initials for the organization. I don't remember it, though it is possibly true. Anyway, he often ignored knockings on the window and complaints for better service. He might have been stone deaf for all the attention he usually gave to the impatient would-be customers. Finally, public clamor brought these scandalous affairs at the post office to the attention of a postal inspector.

Commencement time arrived and I was graduated—barely—with an L.L.B. from the law school. No relief had come about in the post office, and professors were now quite angry. I told Bill good-bye, adding that I expected him to visit me in the summer and that I would return to Ole Miss for a visit with him. His status at the post office was not mentioned by either of us.

Soon after I arrived home in Greenville to practice law in my father's firm, I heard that Bill had quietly been relieved of his position, though efforts had been made to save the job—efforts that went even so far as soliciting the aid of Mississippi U.S. Senator John Sharp Williams, who either refused to help or couldn't do anything about it. Despite rumors, no charges were filed against Bill, and things ended more happily than they might have.

It wasn't long before I had a letter from him, entirely unrepentant. The letter said that he was glad to be out of the hated post office, free to dream and write. It presented a version of the remark he spoke at that time to several people: that he was glad to be no longer at the mercy of any "son of a bitch" who had two cents, but the letter used four lines of fittingly varied lengths instead of the four possibly objectionable words, another example of his reticence about off-color language, even in a letter to a friend.

A new life was to begin that summer for both of us.

Greenville

When Faulkner first visited me in my town, Greenville was a peaceful, neighborly community, set on the Mississippi River, with levees on both the Mississippi and Arkansas sides constructed in the optimistic hope of preventing the great stream from inundating the land. Grandly described by the Chamber of Commerce at the beginnings of the 1920s as the "Queen City of the Delta," it was the largest town in the Mississippi Delta. Even so, the population was only a bit more than seventeen thousand, over 50 percent being black.

My entry into my father's law firm, Wynn and Wasson, in 1921 was made without fanfare or the sounding of trumpets by either the citizenry or the Washington County Bar Association. Wynn and Wasson rarely dealt in criminal cases, much to my disappointment, and civil suits were concerned with real estate deals, contracts, equities, dignified divorce cases (these reluctantly), legacies, and so forth, none of which seemed exciting to me. The few cases thrown my way to be dealt with in justice-of-the-peace courts seemed dull affairs. It was soon evident that I wasn't cut out to be a successful, or even proficient, attorney-at-law, which was a great disappointment, I'm sure, to my father. However, he never expressed such feelings and was patient with and tolerant of me.

William Alexander Percy, already established as a nationally known poet, was a partner in the law firm of Percy, Straus and Percy, whose offices were in the same building as those of Wynn and Wasson. Will encouraged me to continue writing poetry and also let me read and criticize many of his own new verses. Faulkner had written a critical review of one of Will's books of verses in an issue of *The Mississippian*. It was a savage review, more or less to Will's displeasure. Will felt that Faulkner had assumed a rather lofty and supercilious air in his piece.

Sometimes when Bill enclosed new verses in letters, I showed them to Will Percy. Will did not care for them. He considered them superficial in manner and content and too imitative of what so many other poets had already written. He said that Faulkner had talent, that the poems were "youthfully sensual," and that with the passage of time Faulkner probably would mature. I considered Will to be a wise mentor and I was flattered by his friendship. He was an older man—about thirty-five when I first met him—and a distinguished and wealthy one, who, with his father, former U.S. Senator LeRoy Percy, was owner of a large cotton plantation. Will was also a splendid pianist. We often played duets—his father's poker playing crowd must have found our music an annoyance—I at the violin, he at the piano. Practicing law became bearable to me because of Will Percy's friendship and counseling.

Into this milieu William Faulkner came to visit me in my family's home, and I sometimes visited him at Ole Miss. It was a period of our friendship that would end for us, in the spring of 1927, with the great flood of the Mississippi River.

My family was composed of Father, Mother, my sister Mary (who had married a Louisiana sugar planter and lived on his plantation near Baton Rouge), another sister, Lady Ree, my brother, Rhodes, who was ten years younger than

I, and Ruth, who was only four years old when Bill first met her and became enamored of her.

Immediately upon meeting him, each member of the Wasson family accepted Bill, and his visits at our house lasted from two or three days to two weeks.

The first time Bill came, Will Percy invited us to his house for an afternoon of tennis. Will's tennis court was the finest in Greenville. That afternoon Bill was in one of his Bohemian moods and wasn't wearing shoes or socks. Although it was generally accepted for children to wander around town barefoot, it was not so for adults. Barefoot or shod, Bill followed his own codes of behavior and did as he pleased so long as he did not hurt anyone. Mother thought it was absurd of him to go about without shoes, but she never told him so. She simply put his conduct down as harmless and eccentric.

On the afternoon we were to go to Will's, Bill had been at a jug of corn whiskey. He thought he had it well hidden in his valise, though I am sure Mother knew he had it with him, because she handed him a mint as we headed toward the excuse of an automobile Bill had recently purchased. It was an outlandish roadster and he was very proud of it.

"Well, Bill," Mother said, giving him the mint, "aren't you and Ben going to play tennis?"

"Yessum," he said.

"You've forgotten your shoes, haven't you?"

"No'm, I just like to play tennis barefooted."

"Oh," Mother said, "I see," and paused. "Don't you want another mint to take with you."

I was relieved when he said good-bye and we drove away. "Can't anybody fool Mrs. Wasson," he said.

"I don't try," I said.

The Percy house was by far the most impressive resi-

The Wasson family's house, Greenville

dence in Greenville. It wasn't a mansion, but it had a
rather grand air about it—two stories, soft yellow stucco
with a pillared porch. The overall effect was one of
spaciousness. There were Lombardy poplars lining a side
of the house, with the tennis court slightly to the rear.
When we arrived I saw that Will had invited several young
women and men to play or watch the games. Will was at
the curb to meet us as we stepped from the car.

When I introduced the two poets, I felt that they immediately disliked each other. I knew by the polite but cool
way Will acknowledged the introduction that he didn't
"cotton-up" to Bill. Also, the way Will squinted his marvelous blue eyes at me said volumes. Bill merely nodded to
him.

"You're in time, Mr. Faulkner, to try a twosome with
me, if you don't object too much to an inferior partner."

Bill mumbled a reply. Will glanced questioningly at me,

then moved with his guest toward the court, pausing and introducing Bill to the other guests.

Though it could not be described as a success, at least the game was mercifully brief. Only moments after the first balls had been lobbed across the net, Bill began to play badly. He lumbered about attempting to hit the ball; he lunged, lost his balance, and fell. Two men rushed to help him, and he seemed dazed as he got to his feet.

"I don't believe your friend feels very well, Ben," Will called to me from the court. "Maybe you'd better take him for a drive."

Faulkner heard Will's remark. "Yes, sir, I don't feel very well. My bad leg is hurting a lot," he said, referring to the flying injury he claimed to have received in Canada.

We immediately left the small crowd. I offered to take the wheel, but Bill insisted that he drive.

Thus occurred the meeting between my two first poet-mentors, neither of whom ever learned to like the other. Faulkner never referred to that game of tennis, and I, needless to say, didn't either.

After Bill had departed for Ole Miss the next day, Will and I were having our customary Coke, and Will laughed and said, "Lucky he didn't break a leg. It's probably true that the Lord does look after drunks."

Mother and Bill Faulkner got along wonderfully well. There was between them a true rapport, despite many extraordinary disparities. Conversationally, they were congenial. Mother, with Bill, showed overtones of light banter. He bore an air of superior courtesy. Father was friendly with my guest, but he eyed him a bit askance, caring nothing about poetry or contemporary literature. His favorite and "most modern" author was Mark Twain, for whom Bill also held a high esteem and about whom they

William Alexander Percy

once talked. Father was a realist. Mother was a romantic. She had a few women friends, but her heart wasn't in a close relationship with them.

Faulkner was chivalrous toward all women, regardless of age. With them, from the youngest to the oldest, there was a suggestion in his manner that he wore a plume in his hat. (Contrary to the customs of other men of that time, he never wore a hat, even when convention called for it.)

Mother sometimes teased Bill, and he plainly enjoyed her playful, mildly flirtatious ways. He knew, too, that she never probed into his private life. With us he was content to stay around the house, to write, read, or take rides in the automobile. It distressed Mother that he did not want to attend the social functions of the young people, either formal or informal ones.

Once when there was to be a large dance at the Elysian Club, the center of Greenville's "society" affairs, Bill was invited to attend as my guest. Young people from all parts of the Delta were to attend, and W. C. Handy's blues band was to play for the function. I knew that Bill liked Handy's music, and this might induce him to accept the invitation. When Mother learned that Bill did not wish to attend, she went directly to his bedroom, knocked on the door, and was invited in. She said she apologized if she were "butting in his business," but she hoped he would go. He said he didn't care to and that he didn't have the proper clothes. Mother said to leave that to her.

The next morning on the day of the dance she joined him at the table where we were having breakfast together. She rang for a cup of coffee and told Bill that she had obtained a suit for him and that there was no need to protest. Further, she said she had made a date for him with a most attractive young lady, a friend of mine, and that he and I could "double date" for the dance. I looked at Bill and he looked at me, and I think he was amused by Mother's maneuverings and machinations.

"You outfoxed me, Mrs. Wasson, and I reckon since you went to so much trouble, I had better mind you."

The suit fit him. He and I got our dates. We went to the dance together. He didn't dance but liked his date. He didn't drink too much whiskey during the evening, and his date was utterly charmed with him.

Bill Faulkner's gentlemanly code extended to men as well as women. In 1927 my brother Rhodes finished high school and that fall entered Ole Miss. I wrote Bill suggesting that he look after Rhodes. Bill immediately invited Rhodes to have lunch with him at Miss Ella Somerville's popular little tea room, The Tea Hound. In his usual polite manner Bill asked Rhodes to order, which, being young and vigorous, Rhodes did in a big way. Bill ordered only a cup of tea. When lunch was served to Rhodes, Bill nonchalantly pulled a wrapped sandwich from his pocket and carefully placed it on his plate. He possibly had used his last dollar to entertain my brother.

In 1924 Bill reported to me in a letter that his book of poetry, *The Marble Faun,* was to be published because the Four Seas Press of Boston was imperceptive enough to accept it. As is well known, Four Seas was a vanity press in Boston, and Phil Stone had made financial arrangements with them to publish the manuscript. This is yet another example of Bill's straying from facts, harmless enough, perhaps, but hell on a biographer.

He went on to joke in the letter that I should expect to see him soon in Sunday newspaper photos. He said that when all was going well he felt he could be an excellent writer. He added that he had been emotionally upset but had recovered and was doing some writing. He enclosed with the letter a short poem he had written that morning.

Soon another letter arrived in which he asked if I knew a photographer in Greenville who could make a portrait of him to be used in connection with the forthcoming publication of *The Marble Faun*. I made an appointment with Miss Willa Johnson of nearby Lake Washington, and on the proposed date he came to Greenville for a sitting.

Miss Willa was considered to be rather eccentric. Her hair was severely bobbed. She was short and chunky and wore dark and mannishly tailored clothes. Generally, her mannerisms and speech were brusque. It was a widely known fact that she not only indulged in booze but also frequently sat in on poker games, often the only woman playing with a group of men, more than holding her own with the most skillful and toughest opponents. She scorned poker players of her own sex; she smoked cigarettes, not tailor-made ones, but rolled her own.

Bill had arrived in high spirits, still elated that *The Marble Faun* would now be published in the foreseeable future. He firmly believed the book would become a great success both critically and in sales. He did not exactly say so, but he talked of the book as very possibly being the beginning of fame and fortune for him. I was almost as optimistic.

"They're reading poetry again," he said, a moment or so after I introduced them in Miss Willa's "studio," which was the part of her family home made private for her uses. "I believe my book will be an escape for poetry lovers from the scribblings that some authors are presumptuous enough to call poetry."

"Doggerel. I call it *free worse*," Miss Willa punned. They had looked each other over carefully and liked what they saw.

"I got these out to show you," she said, leading us to a table on which were spread in orderly rows photographs of people, white and black, and local scenes—the river, cotton fields, an Indian mound, a tenant cabin. The portraits of blacks struck Faulkner as being exceptionally fine. "Good straight stuff," he said, "nothing fancy here. It's honest."

"Oh, yes, they're good," she said, and they continued to discuss photography, both agreeing that it was one of the true arts, though often bastardized and cheapened by tyros.

As they talked, Miss Willa constantly rolled cigarettes, lighting them with kitchen matches, setting them carelessly down on table edges. Bill had lit up a briar pipe.

"Let's go. We've gabbed enough," she said suddenly. "Stay right where you are," and she moved his head to one side. "That's good. No more jabber." She ducked her head under the black camera cloth and got to work.

From time to time she emerged from under the cloth, leading him to a chair, a window, a sofa, moving his hands in various positions. She worked swiftly and tirelessly for almost an hour.

"That ought to do it," she said finally.

"When will I get them?"

"I ought to have proofs ready in a few days, and since

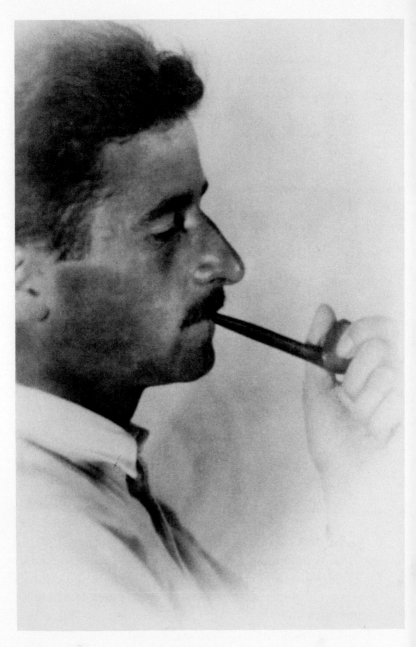

William Faulkner, 1924. Photograph taken by Willa Johnson for promotion of *The Marble Faun*.

you're leaving in the morning, I'll call Ben and he can come by and get proofs of what I think are the good ones and mail them to you. Now you fellows run on, and I'll get to my darkroom. Good-bye. Nice to've met you."

We started for home, strolling slowly along the streets, beneath the spreading limbs of great oak trees. Bill said he had been afraid that Miss Willa might set herself afire when she got under the camera cloth again and again with her lighted cigarettes. "Her camera looked like a kind of Vesuvius, didn't it?" he said. Once during the session, he had warned her about the possibility of the cloth catching on fire.

"Aw, hell and damnation," she had said, "I expect it'll be the death of me, yet." She had declared that she loathed taking pictures of babies, listening to them squall, and hearing the mothers praising "their brats." She had told Bill she'd like to get in a poker game with him sometime, promising she'd "beat the tarnation" out of him and teach him how the game should be played. I'm sorry to say that never occurred, and, many years later, I told him of how Miss Willa had fallen upon very hard days. Near the end of her life she became physically helpless and was placed in the care of some Catholic nurses.

Bill said he hoped she taught the nuns to play poker. Whether she did or didn't I never heard, but the portraits she made pleased him. One of them I sent to *The Record*, the official Sigma Alpha Epsilon national magazine. Bill and I expected that its appearance in the fraternal publication would bring about large numbers of orders for copies of *The Marble Faun*. Our expectations were wildly over optimistic, for the little book was received with indifference by the "brothers" as well as the public at large.

Ruth, my baby sister, was four. She was a very bright little girl, who began talking when only a few months old. She had a rather grave look and even at four carried on a pretty conversation.

Bill Faulkner adored children and, in particular, little girls. I think he envied me because I had three sisters and he had none. His feeling for little girls is evident in *The Sound and the Fury*: Caddy in her muddy drawers and, later, during Quentin's last day at Harvard, when he and the little Italian girl, who speaks no English, walk together, not saying anything to each other.

Bill and Ruth would hold long serious conversations.

I usually rose in the morning before Bill did, went downstairs, and had breakfast with Father, and then we left for the office. One morning I heard Ruth going into Bill's bedroom and then I could hear them talking.

She had climbed into bed with him and had brought with her two pairs of her sister Lady Ree's evening slippers—a pair of silver ones and a pair of gold. I listened to her telling him about them. Then he began to tell her stories about the adventures the slippers had. He gave accounts of castles, princesses, and princes, and invented all kinds of magical happenings, journeys through forests with trees that were silver and gold like the slippers. Ruth was laughing delightedly, and he, now and again, would chuckle with her.

As he was leaving our house and telling Mother goodbye, he handed a folded piece of paper to her. "Here's a poem about Ruth, Mrs. Wasson. Save it and give it to her when she's older and able to understand it."

Years later, after Ruth had married and was living on a cotton plantation near Leland, their home burned to the ground, and they lost everything, including her poem by William Faulkner. I remember two lines: "Your eyes are brown and grave, / And gay is your laughter."

Bill tried working in New York. Occasionally he would visit me, and we corresponded. From Oxford, he wrote me about a book of stories by Sherwood Anderson which he had just read: *Horses and Men*. He said that except for Conrad's "Heart of Darkness" he thought Anderson's "I'm a Fool" the best story he knew. He was surprised that a man Anderson's age could keep the vision and emotion of the young.

After I received that letter, Bill paid us another visit. We regularly took late afternoon walks on the levee. Neither of us ever tired of watching the constantly changing and surging river—tawny, full of angry, churning currents, eager to end the journey to the sea. There was menace in its hurtling motion.

Bill took books along on these walks, and we liked to sit on the soft green grass on the river side of the levee. One afternoon he brought the Anderson book of short stories about which he had written me. Bill read "I'm a Fool" as we sat on the levee embankment. His reading was not very good, since his voice was too low-pitched, with a rather hollow, tinny quality. Yet, he loved reading aloud, and I was a willing, attentive listener. When he had finished "I'm a Fool," he closed the book and put it on the grass beside him.

"By God, that's a man. I'd sho like to meet him and know him."

"Will Percy told me Anderson's in New Orleans now," I said.

"Yes, I heard he is."

"Why don't you go down there and meet him?"

"I've been thinking about it."

We discussed the fact that Elizabeth Prall, for whom Bill had worked in a New York bookstore, was now Mrs. Sherwood Anderson and could introduce Bill to her husband.

"And if you'd go, you'd meet all those writers in *The Double Dealer*, and you could show them some of your stuff."

"It's a good idea. Stone and I talked about it, too, and he thinks I ought to go."

Then he changed the subject and for a while spoke of his poems, of the sad briefness of life, and of the imminence of death. He said again that he had a premonition that he would die young.

We stopped talking and watched the sun set, both of us feeling a reverence for the final moments of its great glowing in the west, then the appearance of the first stars, and the final spasm of color, and soon, darkness, with the willows silhouetted against the darkened sky across the river.

"Listen! You know what that Old Man is saying. 'They're not going to tame me.' And nobody ever will." We went down the levee and through the town and on home for supper.

It wasn't long afterward that I received a short letter from him. The letter has been lost, but I remember that he said, among other things: "I've met Anderson. He's grand. And so is New Orleans."

Bill wrote his first novel, *Soldiers' Pay*, and Anderson sent it to Horace Liveright, who published it. So, maybe, in a somewhat tangential way, the Mississippi River did have something to do with Faulkner's career as a writer. At least, I like to think it did.

Following the publication of *Soldiers' Pay*, I visited the Faulkners in Oxford. Bill had become something of a celebrity, at least in our immediate part of the South. *The Marble Faun* had, of course, been published. Some of his poems had appeared in *The Double Dealer* and *The New Republic* and several of his prose sketches in the New Orleans *Times-Picayune*. Actually, the appearance of *Soldiers'*

Horace Liveright

Pay had brought him more notoriety than celebrity, since many readers deplored much of the book because of its frankness and lurid descriptions, such as a character whose eyes were the color of urine. Faulkner was delighted at their outrage.

He had received galley proofs of his second novel, *Mosquitoes*, a few days before I arrived at Oxford for the visit. He was both pleased and displeased with them. A letter from Horace Liveright accompanied the galleys. This brilliant and sometimes erratic editor wrote that Boni and Liveright couldn't get the book by the censors if some of the passages were not deleted.

"I expect he knows what he's talking about since that's his business," Bill said. "Someday authors will be allowed to write about life truthfully and not be guided by such ignorant vultures as the censors. No hedging with life."

He was upset about the "toning down" of things he espe-

cially liked in the manuscript: the lesbian element and the
suggested incestuousness between the brother and sister.
Also, the publisher had apparently decided to make the
"outdoor privy" part less graphic and vivid. "And ruin it,"
Bill said bitterly.

I was absorbed in rereading the manuscript of *Mosquitoes* when I heard him running up the stairs. He stared
at me from the doorway, his eyes keen, mobile, and birdy.
His cheeks were deeply flushed, and there was that fury in
his eyes. He held out a letter to me.

"All women should be made to do a big tub of washing
every day." he said. "Maybe that way they'd be too busy to
interfere with what other people are doing." I had never
seen him so upset. I asked him to sit down while I read the
letter, which was from his publisher.

According to its contents, Miss Maud had written to
Liveright, accusing the publisher of withholding royalty
payments that were due her son. She had declared that she
knew little or nothing about business matters, but that it
did seem strange to her that he hadn't received more
money. She said further that Bill needed the money and
didn't know anything about financial affairs. Liveright's letter contained a royalty statement from the firm.

When I finished reading, I didn't know what to say to
him.

"She says I don't know anything about business. I do
know how to mind my own. And she thought she was doing
the 'well meaning' thing in writing to them, trying to pro-
tect my interests. Godamighty, fellow, if there's anything
that upsets the world, it's people who do things because
they consider it's 'well meaning.' Oh, hell, I don't expect
it's worth getting so mad and upset, and in such an uproar.
It's done."

"After all," I began, "she is your mother . . ."

"I'm perfectly aware she's my mother," he said coldly.

Then he half-smiled. "Come on, let's get out of the house and take a walk out to Jim Stone's. Let's go before I blow up again."

We took a long walk, and he told me more about his experiences since we had last been together. This was our first meeting since he had gone to New Orleans, met Sherwood Anderson, and had written and sold *Soldiers' Pay*. He also had taken a trip to Europe. He had sent me a postcard telling of being incarcerated briefly for vagrancy. From Paris he had sent me a photograph of himself sporting a beard (Notre Dame Cathedral in the background). As we walked he told how he wrote *Mosquitoes* on the Mississippi Gulf Coast. Then he said he was in love.

"Her name is Helen Baird."

"But I know her," I said. "She came to Sewanee dances, and her brother Pete was with me there. The Bairds are from Nashville."

"Yes," he said. "It's hell being in love, ain't it?"

Helen Baird later became Mrs. Guy Lyman. Her husband had been a fraternity brother of mine at Sewanee.

Helen Baird was, I feel sure, one of the great loves of Bill Faulkner's life, and he never lost his fondness for the Mississippi Gulf Coast where he had known her.

My mother and William Faulkner had many talks on many subjects. Theirs weren't profound or intellectual conversations, since Mother was neither intellectual nor profound. She didn't discuss books with him, since she only cared for light, romantic novels and didn't read nonfiction at all. She told him once that he should write love stories, that they were the ones women preferred, and that, after all, women made up the majority of book readers in the world.

"Maybe they do, but I don't write for readers, I write for myself and because I have to."

Mother shook her head. "To tell the truth, Bill, I

Helen Baird

couldn't read *Soldiers' Pay*. It's way over my head, and what I read was ugly."

"I never said it was pretty, and, anyhow," he grinned at her, "I couldn't read it now, either. So we're even."

The Oldham house in Oxford was a gathering place for young men from the University of Mississippi and the town. It was a rare occasion that co-eds or young town ladies came to these informal drop-ins. One or two of Estelle Oldham's close girl acquaintances might now and then be there. Otherwise, the varying groups were composed of "gentlemen callers," to use the phrase immortalized by Tennessee Williams. They were drawn there as bees are drawn to nectar.

Victoria was the eldest of the three Oldham daughters. Estelle was second, then Dorothy. In 1916, I met the famous Estelle when a group of my SAE friends took me with them on a Sunday afternoon to call on Sally Murry Wilkins,

Bill Faulkner's first cousin. Estelle was the only other girl present that afternoon. I was awed by these two noted favorites, and especially by Estelle, whose popularity had become a legend.

I must have been a rather impossible young man, because that Sunday afternoon I considered myself to be in society's inner and sacred circle. I thought Sally Murry was pretty; I wasn't sure that Estelle was. I did know that I had never before met so "alluring" a woman—she must have then been in her early twenties, since she was a bit older than Bill.

Her body was slim and, like her thin hands, in constant motion. Her eyes were the most vivacious I had ever seen. I couldn't tell you their color, but I know they were animated and sparkling. Her mouth was her least attractive feature, seeming, when pursed up, as it often was, somewhat selfish-looking. She was a lively talker, rarely stopping her chatter, which now and then was mildly malicious. She was flirtatious, a trait she never lost even when she became a much older woman. It was inherent in her nature and was, I'm sure, one of the reasons she was more popular with men than with women. Not that she cared. I suspect she was rather proud of it. She wasn't fond of women.

She was always thoroughly absorbed in whatever a man was saying to her. One would have thought, watching her as she listened to a man, that he was the most fascinating and brilliant creature in the world.

She appeared to be frail. Her dresses were usually frilly and considered marvelously stylish. Even when she was a grandmother, her clothes had an air of extreme femininity, but of course they weren't nearly so frilly as they had been when she had a name for being the "best dressed girl in Mississippi." Altogether, she was seductive.

While I was attending Sewanee, Estelle married. Her

Estelle Oldham, 1913

husband, Cornell Franklin, had graduated from the law school at Ole Miss. Departing from his hometown, Columbus, Mississippi, he became associated with legal work that led him to considerable prominence in Honolulu, where he elected to make a career for himself. Gossips in Oxford said that Mrs. Oldham, being ambitious for Estelle, had brought about the marriage and that Estelle did not love Cornell and that her true love was her childhood sweetheart, Billy Faulkner.

I was unaware in those days that Bill was supposed to have been in love with Estelle. He had rarely mentioned her to me. When I returned to Ole Miss as a law student, she was living in Honolulu, leading—it was said—a glittering social life with her husband. Apparently she had, to Major and Mrs. Oldham's satisfaction, made a brilliant match indeed.

Mrs. Oldham herself exuded warmth and charm in her hospitality. She was a talented pianist and had set a number of poems to music. I wrote the words for an Ole Miss alma mater song, since none existed at that time, and Mrs. Oldham composed the music. Insofar as I know, and fervently hope, this flagrant miscarriage of poetry and music has long since vanished. Bill never mentioned my "Alma Mater," which rather hurt my feelings at the time.

During one of my infrequent trips to see Bill and his family, Estelle happened to be in Oxford for a visit with her family. When she arrived, the townfolk were agog with excitement. She had brought her young daughter, Victoria (nicknamed Cho-Cho), and the child's Japanese nurse, who wore Japanese dress, even to the obi arranged around her waist, complete with large bow in the back. The nurse spoke almost no English. I was nearly spellbound by my first sight of her. She was the first Japanese I had ever seen, with the exception of Sessue Hayakawa, the great actor of the silent screen.

During Estelle's visit, there was constant open house at her parents' home, and Oldham hospitality was extended generously. Major Oldham was a quiet man, rather aloof and reserved, considered by some people to be cold, for after speaking cordially to visitors, he would withdraw. He was a Republican, which made him rather suspect. He was a federal judge and had been called upon to help Bill during Bill's high jinks at the post office.

Estelle Oldham Franklin and her daughter Victoria (Cho-Cho),
Shanghai, about 1924

Estelle was effervescent and welcoming to all who came
to see her. Guests not playing tennis would sit on the
spacious side porch of the Oldham's handsome house, talking and drinking tea served by the tiny Japanese woman. I
suspect, and so did Bill, that several of the male callers,
two in particular who enjoyed reputations for lechery,
made oafish—Bill's adjective—attempts to seduce the ex-
otic lady. Bill told me the ridiculous tale, then current, that
oriental women were sexually different from occidental
women, being "made on the bias."

When I called at the Oldhams', Bill remained at home,
finishing a poem. I had a delightful afternoon and stayed on
late. The visitors had all departed, and Cho-Cho and nurse
were upstairs. Estelle and I were alone.

Saying that she wanted to play the piano, she invited me
into the house, to what Mrs. Oldham called the music
room. Estelle began playing popular pieces, and I stood

behind her humming the tunes she played and turning the pages. She finished a piece, then rose from the piano stool, put her arms around my shoulders, and we spontaneously kissed. As we stood there embracing and kissing, Cho-Cho came into the room so quietly we hadn't heard her. Then she called out to her mother, and Estelle and I quickly broke away. Cho-Cho held out her arms, and Estelle picked her up, and I left the house as quickly as I could get away. (Conventionally, it is ungentlemanly of me to tell this story, but it has a direct bearing on a piece of Faulkner's writing.)

I walked through the Oxford twilight for a while, and, when it was near darkness, I went slowly to the Faulkner house.

"Get lost in the great metropolis, did you?" Bill said.

I mumbled that I hadn't been lost; then I blurted out what had occurred in the Oldhams' music room. I told him I was fearful of the consequences and what Estelle would think about it. I was very concerned that Cho-Cho might prattle.

He was quiet after I finished the story. "Watch out," he finally said, "and remember, Bud, that Eve wasn't the only woman who handed out an apple, just the first one." Then he gave me the poem he had finished while I was away. I read it, and he never afterward said anything about the incident with Estelle.

He did not forget it, though, as I shall show.

The greatest flood in the recorded history of the Mississippi River occurred in 1927, when the levee broke on April 22, several miles above Greenville. The flood waters covered nearly all of the Mississippi Delta, remaining until so late in the spring that very little cotton was planted that season. Indeed, Bill had been correct when he had told me the river said, "They're not going to tame me." A personal result of the flood for me was that I decided to go to New York City to seek another career. I didn't see Bill again before I left Mississippi. While Greenville was under water, a postcard from him expressed the hope that "Greenville and you will soon dry out."

And so I became a New Yorker and began a wholly new life and career. My moving to New York would considerably alter my life. It would affect Bill's also.

New York

On MacDougal Street immediately across from the house in which I had a room was the Provincetown Theatre. The theater is still there, but the little house has long since been demolished to clear a space for New York University buildings. I thought when I became an occupant of that room that I had become a genuine Greenwich Villager. When Bill first saw it, he remarked, "Ah, the Bohemian life!"

When I moved into the house, it was also the domain of mice, rats, cockroaches, and bed bugs, and it was, literally, lousy. But I was proud of being a tenant. My room on the second floor was overcrowded with haphazard furniture, abandoned by former occupants. An enormous bed filled most of the wall space on one side. In showing me the room, the landlord, who was famous for his leniency regarding delinquent rent payment, demurred when I mentioned the overlarge bed, sat on it, and bounced up and down. "Young man, it is a big bed made for making love," he said beaming.

The single window opposite the bed overlooked a courtyard surrounded by tall buildings on Washington Square. In the open space were two dusty, wretched specimens of heaven trees. My mother and father and my sister Mary Wilkinson and her husband were outraged that I lived in that house and neighborhood. Mary wept and called the room disgusting, but I ignored the family objections.

In the summer of 1928, while I was working in New York on what I hoped would be a novel, Bill wrote me from Oxford that he had completed a manuscript called *Flags in the Dust*. To his almost overwhelming disappointment Horace Liveright's firm had rejected the new work and strongly discouraged him from attempting to sell it elsewhere. Bill refused to give up efforts to place it with a publisher and asked me to try to sell it. He lacked the money, he said, to pay the postage for shipping it to prospective publishers. The letter was somewhat a wail of distress to a friend. Although I had no experience as a literary agent, I wrote suggesting that he send the manuscript to me and said I'd make every effort to find a publisher for him.

My contacts with publishers and their editors were few. The only one who I felt might be of real help was Herschel Brickell, a former Mississippian who was an editor at Henry Holt and Son. He and Norma, his wife, had generously befriended me. When I explained my dilemma to Herschel, he gave me a list of people who might be interested in the manuscript. As soon as *Flags in the Dust* arrived, I read it and I considered it a splendid job of writing.

As I read it, I was startled when I came to a part that told of Belle Mitchell and Horace Benbow interrupted by little Belle's unexpected entrance when they are kissing in the music room of the Mitchell house.

I was struggling with my own manuscript, *The Devil Beats His Wife*, but, postponing my plan to go to Woodstock to write, I began peddling the Faulkner manuscript. Brickell rejected it for Holt, and after I had submitted it to nine other publishers, he suggested I give it to Harrison Smith, the Harcourt, Brace editor. Since in those days I was incredibly casual about making appointments, I took *Flags* to Smith, who came to the reception room to see me when the receptionist informed him that I had been sent by Herschel Brickell.

I told him about the manuscript. He said he had read and admired *Soldiers' Pay* but was unfamiliar with *Mosquitoes*. I handed him the manila envelope containing *Flags* and requested a quick decision from him. I then felt free to go on to Woodstock, but I gave him the address where I might be reached.

A few weeks went by in that quiet colony of authors, musicians, actors, and other creative folk, and I nearly completed my manuscript. As I was making arrangements to return to New York, a letter came from Hal Smith, asking me to see him in his office the following Monday. The letter was quickly followed by another from him asking me to come on Tuesday because he had forgotten that Monday was Labor Day. I promptly and eagerly appeared at Harcourt, Brace inasmuch as Smith's letters implied definite interest in *Flags*. He came to the reception room, blinked behind his thick lenses, quirked his mouth in his characteristic way, and said, "Wasson, this is a damn good manuscript you've written."

Flabbergasted, I reminded him that when I talked to him about *Soldiers' Pay*, I had pointed out that William Faulkner was also the author of *Flags*.

"Now I remember our talk, but the title page was missing and I remembered your mentioning a manuscript of your own. I like this one. The man's good. I'd like to say right now we'll publish it, but Alf Harcourt has also read it and has some reservations. Let's go in and talk to him. He's expecting us."

He led the way to Harcourt's office and introduced me to him. The upshot of our conversation that day was that Harcourt felt the manuscript needed shortening about twenty-five percent. He also had a feeling that its author would be unable to sacrifice so much of the manuscript. If they accepted it, he'd like for me to do the editing, and he'd need it done in about two weeks so that he could include it on Harcourt, Brace's forthcoming list. I said that I would cut the manuscript, and we agreed on a fee of fifty dollars for me and a three-hundred-dollar advance to the author. He stated that he did not wish the author to take part in the editing. With excitement, I began working immediately.

Bill Faulkner's *Flags in the Dust* was the first novel manuscript I had ever attempted to edit, but I felt capable of doing the job. Bill replied to my telegram, delighted that I had consummated a sale for him. He said he had decided to come on to New York and asked me to meet him at Pennsylvania Station.

A few days later I saw his short figure coming up the stairway at the station. He was carrying a satchel, wearing a raincoat, and carrying a golf bag filled with clubs. As he ascended the stairs, I wondered where he expected to play golf. In Central Park?

The great city's noise surrounded us as he stretched out his hand and smiled. "Bud, I sho am glad you met me at the dee-po."

I don't remember where he stayed during that time in New York. I didn't have room for him of course, but I seem to recall that he stayed in a small hotel in the Village, which he had likely known when he worked briefly years before in the Manhattan book shop managed by Elizabeth Prall. Stark Young, a friend of both, had introduced them. When we reached Sheridan Square and left the subway, he told me that he would see me the next morning, and we parted.

The day following his arrival we went to the Harcourt, Brace offices. I introduced him to Hal, and there was immediate rapport between the pair. In Harcourt's office, we were introduced first to Louise Bonino, Harcourt's private

Stark Young

secretary, and then Hal introduced Bill to Harcourt. These two were friendly enough, but no real warmth was established between them.

Harcourt got right down to business and inquired about my progress with the cutting and told Bill that he doubted that he could do a good job of deleting material from his own manuscript.

"Yes, sir, you're right," Bill said. "It's hard enough losing all that sweat I pour into writing it down. To have to commit surgery on it would be like losing blood, I reckon."

Harcourt assured Bill that he felt when I finished that it would be a first-class work of fiction. Bill naturally bridled a little at that, and the meeting came to an end.

Staying on in New York for a while, Bill took the opportunity to spend as much time as he could with two friends from the New Orleans days—Bill Spratling, the artist with whom he had accomplished the French Quarter book,

Sherwood Anderson and Other Famous Creoles, and with whom he had gone to Europe, and Lyle Saxon, genial author of *Fabulous New Orleans* and other works and stories. He also frequently saw Owen Crump and Jim Devine. I went about with them to speakeasies in the Village, but I didn't attempt to keep up with Bill's activities.

At times it was difficult for me to pare the *Flags* manuscript. Bill was working on a new novel, but he came to my room almost every day. He never questioned me about what I was deleting or about how my own manuscript was moving along. Mine was at a standstill, since the two-week deadline I had been given on *Flags* left me little or no time for anything else.

I was sticking as closely as I could to the Sartoris family storyline, but I knew it was obligatory to include the Snopeses, Benbows, MacCallums, and others in *Flags*. It was grievous to omit anything. I still felt, though, that the manuscript comprised several novels. It was the first time Yoknapatawpha County had appeared in Faulkner's novels.

In his manuscript there was one short bit of writing that especially attracted me. It is the author's passage describing the mule. I felt that it was out of context, but I could not omit it:

> Round and round the mule went, setting its narrow, deer-like feet delicately down in the hissing cane-pith, its neck bobbing limber as a section of rubber hose in the collar, with its trace-galled flanks and flopping, lifeless ears, and its half-closed eyes drowsing venomously behind pale lids, apparently asleep with the monotony of its own motion. Some Cincinnatus of the cotton fields should contemplate the lowly destiny, some Homer should sing the saga, of the mule and of his place in the South. He it was, more than any one creature or thing, who, steadfast to the land when all else faltered before the hopeless juggernaut of circumstance, impervious to conditions that broke men's hearts because of his venomous and patient preoccupation with the immediate present, won the

prone South from beneath the iron heel of Reconstruction and taught it pride again through humility and courage through adversity overcome; who accomplished the well-nigh impossible despite hopeless odds, by sheer and vindictive patience. Father and mother he does not resemble, sons and daughters he will never have; vindictive and patient (it is a known fact that he will labor ten years willingly and patiently for you, for the privilege of kicking you once); solitary but without pride, self-sufficient but without vanity; his voice is his own derision. . . . Ugly, untiring and perverse, he can be moved neither by reason, flattery, nor promise of reward; he performs his humble monotonous duties without complaint, and his meed is blows. Alive, he is haled through the world, an object of general execration; unwept, unhonored and unsung, he bleaches his awkward, accusing bones among rusting cans and broken crockery and worn-out automobile tires on lonely hillsides, while his flesh soars unawares against the blue in the craws of buzzards.

I told Bill I couldn't bear to omit the eloquent purplish passage. "I'm glad," he said. "I reckon if you did leave it out I'd bear it, but I'd surely hate to see it go."

Finally, when the manuscript was cut as I felt it should be, he read it. "You've done a good job," he said, "and it ought to suit them."

Apparently it met with approval. After it was properly proofread, Hal sent it to the printers.

The morning after I completed my work, and after a night of mild celebration, Bill came to my room as usual, though this time somewhat earlier than had become his custom. He didn't greet me with his softly spoken "good morning" but merely tossed a large obviously filled envelope on the bed. "Read this one, Bud," he said. "It's a real son of a bitch."

I removed the manuscript and read the title on the first page: *The Sound and the Fury*.

"This one's the greatest I'll ever write. Just read it," he said, and abruptly left.

The next morning he again arrived. I had stayed up late, enthralled with his magnificent new manuscript. It left me emotionally stirred for many hours. After telling him so, I said that the sheer technical outrageousness and freshness of the Benjy section made it hard to follow. He said he knew that it was demanding.

"If I could only get it printed the way it ought to be with different color types for the different times in Benjy's section recording the flow of events for him, it would make it simpler, probably. I don't reckon, though, it'll ever be printed that way, and this'll have to be the best, with the italics indicating the changes of events."

He was planning to leave the next day for Oxford. He asked me to take the manuscript to Hal Smith, since he was afraid to leave it in his or my place. He asked that Hal give him a quick decision. And he also requested that I take some watercolor sketches he had painted for possible use on the jacket of *Sartoris*, the name either he, Hal, or I had suggested as the title to replace *Flags in the Dust*. The sketches showed different versions of a black plowing with a mule, the earth being turned over, and, overhead, a blue-washed sky. It was a rather colorful job, but Harcourt, much to Bill's regret, did not accept it. When I delivered the manuscript of *Sound*, Hal ordered that it be placed in a safe.

On what was supposedly Bill's last night in New York during that visit, a few of us celebrated again. We were always celebrating something or other: an arrival, a departure, a completed picture, a just-finished book or story, or the sale of a poem or manuscript.

On this night, I noticed Bill's body had become less slim and he was wearing his moustache thicker than usual. Throughout the years, he kept his hair about the same length, but from time to time he altered the style of his moustache and occasionally grew a beard.

I left the celebration earlier than the others, either because I wanted to do some polishing on my own manuscript or because I had imbibed too much white wine. In the morning, I was awakened by a faint tapping on the door. I opened it and Bill came in, his expression woebegone.

"I got my pocket picked or lost my pocketbook," he said, and turned his back to me. "Kick me." He turned to me again. "Anyhow, it's vanished. I wonder if you'd go with me to see Hal and try to get him to let me have money enough to get back to Mississippi?"

Hal was amused by the story. Lyle Saxon and Bill Spratling felt that Bill should have an extra amount of money for his train ride south, and they scrounged around and fattened his new wallet.

As I bade him good-bye at the station, he thanked me and said: "Let me know about *The Sound and the Fury*. I'm counting on that one."

Now to squeeze together as closely as I can—and without too much verbosity—events that took place before Bill and I were together again. These events had a great bearing on our relationship and the future of his career as a writer.

Just before Christmas, 1928, Hal Smith broke away from Harcourt, Brace, and, with the English publisher, Jonathan Cape, formed a new firm, Cape and Smith. The departure of Smith from Harcourt was not pleasant. It left ripples of discord and enmity in its wake. Harcourt was particularly incensed at the departure of Louise Bonino, who was to become a mainstay of the new firm.

At Hal's suggestion, I moved from my room on Mac-Dougal Street and visited him and his wife Clare and their son and daughter in their brownstone uptown. Hal offered me a job as editor with Cape and Smith, and I accepted with the understanding that I could spend Christmas in Greenville.

While I was in Greenville, Harcourt forwarded the galley proofs of *The Devil Beats His Wife*, which Hal had accepted for Harcourt as one of his final editorial acts there. Reading the proofs of my book and with the unforgettable memory of the recently read *The Sound and the Fury*, I came to the conclusion that I probably would never write another novel, knowing that anything I wrote would be shockingly inferior to Bill's work.

Upon my return to New York there was a new apartment waiting for me. Under Clare and Hal's supervision the top floor of the brownstone that was to house Cape and Smith had been attractively prepared: one large studio-like room for my office and bedroom, a bath, and provision for light cooking. The furnishings were what was then considered quite modern and functional—low slung couch and long table, plus book shelves already filled with books. It was a tremendous improvement over my MacDougal Street room, and I considered everything to be perfect.

Hal's office on the second floor was a comfortable, unpretentious one, and he often came to the third floor to discuss things with me. The staff was small, and all of us were informal with one another—except, of course, with Mr. Cape when he was in this country.

One of Hal's first talks with me was about the manuscript of *The Sound and the Fury*. "If it's as marvelous as you say it is, I want it for our first list," he said. So I went to Harcourt, Brace, where it was released to me because they had decided it was too poor a publishing risk. They also informed me of the approaching date for the release of both *Sartoris* and *The Devil Beats His Wife*, both novels being

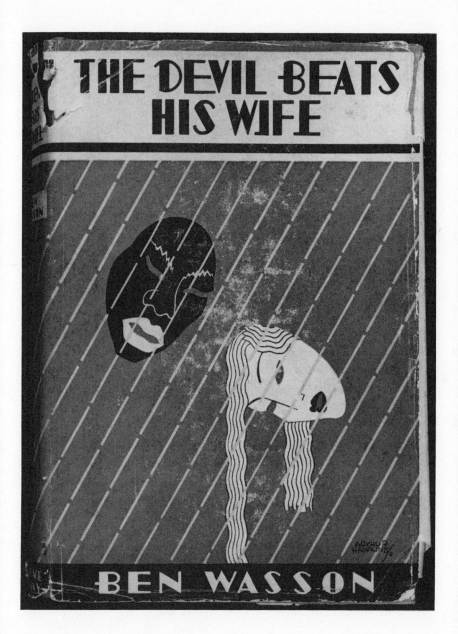

Jacket of Ben Wasson's novel

in final production stages. (The novels were released almost simultaneously. Critics were not overly kind and certainly not ecstatic about either of them, nor did either book sell at all well. And, irony of ironies, mine was treated better critically than Faulkner's.)

The dust jacket of my book was designed by Arthur Hawkins, Jr., who also did many jackets for Bill's later books, and the two men became fairly close friends. On the dust jacket of my novel, this promotion for *Sartoris* appeared:

> These people will, as time moves by, be succeeded by the more worldly and pushing Snopes family. A hint is already given here of that victory without battle when peanut farmers supersede a fine Southern tradition. But now we have before us—both white and black, for even negroes associated with the family take on their characteristics. Mr. Faulkner has painted a big canvas with many fine portraits.

Hal placed the manuscript of *The Sound and the Fury* in the capable hands of Robert Ballou, technical manager, who, as soon as possible, sent it to a printer. The printer returned galley proofs, and Hal grew more excited about the novel. Lenore Marshall, who was in the editorial department, thought it an extraordinary piece of writing and fell in with the small group of admirers.

Then I had a new idea. Evelyn Scott, a distinguished though unconventional lady from Tennessee, whose novels are now sadly neglected and mostly forgotten, was a blue ribbon author on the first list of Cape and Smith. Her big novel about the Civil War, *The Wave*, led the list, and Hal persuaded the prestigious Literary Guild to announce it as one of its choices. The guild's imprimatur added great distinction to any book, fiction or nonfiction. I suggested to Hal that he have Miss Scott read the gallery proof and give us her opinion. My hunch was that she would like it. Hal readily agreed, so after telephoning, I took it to her.

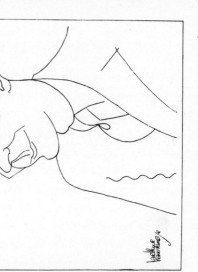

Caricature of Ben Wasson by Arthur Hawkins, designer of jackets for some of Faulkner's books and for Wasson's novel.

SARTORIS

By

WILLIAM FAULKNER

This novel is the portrayal of a family. Impatient and violent, the men have gone out to battle and returned to their homes. There are scarcely any words of fighting spoken by them, yet they have brought back to the Sartoris-by-marriage women the smell of cannon fire and the wounds of their hearts. These women must bear with them, heal them, and smile to themselves a little at the childishness of all men folk. Through the close-knit story runs a sinister thread; there is meanness and fatality, but also life, color, and a quiet and sometimes almost hilarious humor, with a Sartoris always topmost in the pattern.

These people will, as time moves by, be succeeded by the more worldly and pushing Snopes family. A hint is already given here of that victory without battle when peanut farmers supersede a fine southern tradition. But now we have them before us—both white and black, for even negroes associated with the family take on their characteristics. Mr. Faulkner has painted a big canvas with many fine portraits.

Harcourt, Brace and Company
383 MADISON AVENUE, NEW YORK

Promotional copy for *Sartoris* that appeared on back flap of *The Devil Beats His Wife*.

Caricature of William Faulkner by Arthur Hawkins

She lived in a crummy—a kind adjective—two-room place on Hudson Street with trucks roaring by night and day. The room in which I visited her was full of empty and sour-smelling milk bottles and opened tin cans. Papers and books were strewn on chairs, tables, and the unmade bed. She cleared a place for me to sit, not apologizing at all for the condition of her quarters. I looked at her. She was thin, and her most distinguished features were her fine large eyes and her radiant smile. Her voice and manners were still Southern. We talked for a while about Faulkner, and she seemed intensely absorbed in what I told her about him.

"I'll read it right away and write you what I think of it," she told me as our interview ended.

In a few days, a messenger brought me a package containing the *Sound* galleys. When I extracted them and read her enclosed letter, I rushed downstairs to Hal's office with it. Her enthusiastic and understanding remarks also excited Hal. He rubbed his nose and squinted his eyes at me: "Go see her again and thank her for this fine letter. See if she won't write more in detail about the second part of the manuscript. She seems to skimp over it."

"That'll be a lot of trouble for Miss Scott," I said.

"If her additional comments are as penetrating, tell her we'll make all of it into a handsome pamphlet, of course featuring her as its author, and we'll distribute it with the compliments of Cape and Smith to critics and book dealers and send it out with our salesmen. Go telephone her now. We'll talk money later."

That's what I did and what Evelyn Scott did and what Hal Smith did, and it all added up to a fine publicity brochure, tastefully designed by Arthur Hawkins and disseminated as Hal suggested.

Miss Scott's superb critique was deeply appreciated by

Faulkner when I sent him a copy, and it constituted, as far as I know, the first understanding coverage of that work. It was the first that seemed to give a serious damn about him.

I read the galley proofs of *Sound* before forwarding them to Bill. I was reading mostly for typographical errors and misspellings. In reading the Benjy section I arrogantly and heedlessly and, yes, ignorantly, decided I could improve the method of telling and do something about the italics. I don't recall what I did, but when Bill received the proofs he wrote me an angry letter, asking that the section be set in type as he had indicated and written it, with no more tampering on my part. Obviously and plainly he was indignant with me. Later he wrote a less harsh letter about the matter, but this was the first time I had been on the receiving end of his lightning bolts of wrath.

I wasn't stupid enough to try to defend what I had done, and when Bill wrote me that he knew I meant well, he couldn't have put it more scathingly. It was, though, the only unpleasantness between us, and neither of us, in the years that followed, ever referred to it.

The Sound and the Fury was published in the autumn of 1929. It stirred no clarion trumpet. It was, in fact, shrugged off by many critics. One made the cruel and obvious comment that the *Macbeth* phrase from which the title had been taken should have been concluded, "signifying nothing."

Bill could only feel bitter that the novel met with such skimpy attention. He later admitted to me that the slight had indeed wounded him and that he believed an author could stand anything more easily than cold indifference. He frequently communicated with me while I was at Cape and Smith. The letters he wrote me there have been taken by someone, and now and then one or another of them will appear in a book or an article. I don't know who removed the letters from the Cape and Smith files. I suppose it doesn't really matter that they now and then surface mysteriously.

Bill and Estelle had married. And, after living somewhere in Oxford for a while, they bought a large run-down pre-Civil War house and several surrounding acres and named the house Rowanoak; later they spelled it Rowan Oak. They had fine restoration plans for the property. Bill was pressed for money as usual, but he wrote: "I am content and I am happy. Right now all the bells in the world seem to be ringing for me." That, at least, was the substance of his letter.

In yet another letter to me, he made, as far as I know, a first and certainly startling, revelation about *Sanctuary*, not, however, mentioning it by title. I suppose it was his way of making a one-line outline of the plot of a book yet to be written: "I am writing a story about a girl who gets raped with a corncob."

I read it to Hal, who peered at me over his glasses and said, "Good God, I'd be thrown in jail if I published anything like that. But I'll publish it undoubtedly. Tell him to go ahead and write it."

The Welsh author Richard Hughes was in New York to enjoy the acclaim of his novel, *The Innocent Voyage*. Published as *A High Wind in Jamaica* in England it had been a great success there. I met Hughes at several literary shebangs. He visited the Cape and Smith offices now and then and came to my apartment. He had a reddish beard. Ladies considered him to be very handsome, magnetic, and masculine—a way of saying they thought he was sexy. Men also liked him. He wasn't a highbrow, bookish type and didn't talk one's ear off (as Thomas Wolfe did me when he spent an afternoon in my room). One night I answered

Rowan Oak, 1931

William Faulkner, Rowan Oak, 1931

the ring of the doorbell downstairs and it was Hughes. I invited him in, and we went upstairs to my rooms, where I fixed us drinks.

He was a delightful, colorful, graphic, and wide-ranging conversationalist. He talked about New York, but the whole United States fascinated him. He asked me what author I considered the best in this country. Without hesitating I said William Faulkner. I suggested that he read *Soldiers' Pay* to begin with, then *Sartoris*, and he might glance through *Mosquitoes*, which I was not truly enthusiastic about.

Upon his return to London, Hughes recommended Bill's books to Chatto and Windus, who immediately made a contract for *Soldiers' Pay*. Jonathan Cape had read the Faulkner novels but evinced no interest in them for his British firm. Published in England, Bill had a fine critical reception, and reviews by Arnold Bennett and others bounced back across the Atlantic Ocean and were read and heeded by American critics.

The reception Bill received in England boosted his morale, and for the first time he began to be taken seriously in this country; at least an impetus to read his books was created here.

My job at Cape and Smith came to an end. I moved on to an agency for actors and authors, the American Play Company. It was a quite distinguished old firm and, for a long time, had been under the aegis of its founder, a New York society woman, Elizabeth Marbury. The firm was considered for a while to be snobbish. When I went there to head the literary department, John Rumsey was the titular head of the firm, but the real mover and shaker of the organization was Leland Hayward.

Before I went to the American Play Company and while I was still with Cape and Smith, I had regularly attended meetings of the Friday Culture Club—it met on Thursdays! Among its members were fun-loving editors, authors, actors, song writers, and other major and minor celebrities who took their professions seriously enough but who could escape stodginess through the club and its informal lunches. Charles Behan, of the American Play Company, was a regular. He spoke to Leland about me. Leland and I made an appointment, and almost immediately I joined his firm as manager of the writers' department.

I wish that someday a fuller piece would be written about the Friday Culture Club. Its career was brief and raffish; its members ruthless with sacred cows and filled with fun and humor. Famous folks were members, such as Ripley, originator of "Believe It or Not," and Frank Buck, whose newspaper feature, "Bring 'em Back Alive" was widely read throughout the country. Bill attended one meeting but was not amused; he called it "much too gabby."

Under the guidance of the extraordinary, exuberant Hayward, the American Play Company was beginning to reshape its image. His unorthodox and very personal way of operating the firm appealed to most of the clients, who were far from being the stuffed shirts who at one time had made up the roster.

The literary department had fallen into desuetude. I found very few manuscripts. There was one by Somerset Maugham, a travel piece that excited me when I came across it, but it had been sent around to magazine editors until it was dog-eared. Leland realized that he wasn't offering me much, but soon in his lively way, he led me to popular and up-and-coming writers.

This somewhat peripatetic preamble to the American Play Company is not out of place, since my employment there determined much of Faulkner's future and mine also.

Sanctuary was to be published soon. Bill already had checked the first set of galley proofs, which, largely at his own expense, he rewrote. I read the first galleys and told Hayward about them. No one in the office agreed with him when he said that the story of *Sanctuary* had motion picture possibilities. Movie rights particularly interested Hayward since Hollywood was where the big money lay in the agency business.

At that time "The Town Crier" was Alexander Woollcott's weekly radio program. He attracted a large following as a drama critic and as a contributor to *The New Yorker*. He commented on matters that struck his fancy, his "fancy fancy," I should say.

In that circusy radio program, Woollcott was his own ringmaster, and he cracked his whip as he chose. He was feared by actors and writers and musical composers, some of whom shamefully pandered to him.

Shortly before the publication of *Sanctuary*, I obtained Woollcott's private telephone number. I screwed up my courage and called him and left word with his secretary to have The Gentleman phone me at his leisure. I not at all casually mentioned the names of several of our common friends and acquaintances—Marc Connelly, Frank Sullivan, Russel Crouse, and others. I also mentioned *Sanctuary*. Apparently I obtained the desired results, for Woollcott's secretary telephoned me the next day to say that he'd take a peek at the book, and, if he liked it, would mention it on a future "Town Crier." "People clamor, you know," she said, "to be mentioned on Mr. Woollcott's program."

Almost simultaneously with the publication of *Sanctuary*, Woollcott not only mentioned it, but devoted almost his entire program to the novel, singing praises as only he could sing them. He vowed it was a monstrous tale, a true gothic spellbinder, a work of possible genius certain to chill the marrow of its readers' bones. He predicted a great future for, as I recall his saying, "one William Faulkner."

I was in the studio listening to and watching Woollcott as he broadcast the program, the script held before him, his mouth close to the microphone, his spectacles giving him an owlish appearance, an impression he cultivated.

As I was leaving the studio, he took me by an elbow and led me into the elevator.

"My astounding and incredible memory and my famous extrasensory perception inform me that you are Wasson, the unabashed promotor of Master Faulkner! Come, let's repair to the nearest oasis and imbibe the mead of the godless." He hailed a cab and we went to a speakeasy where he plied me with questions about Faulkner. I had heard he was notoriously merciless and noted for his chutzpah, and he was asking me highly intimate questions about his favorite new author. I fielded some of the more ruthless ones as well as I could, certainly all those questions regarding Bill's sex life.

"If the young genius comes to this Sodom and Gomorrah, you are to introduce him to me," he commanded. "If you fail me, you'll find yourself in my gem-encrusted dog house." He chuckled. "Now, don't forget."

I had no idea that Bill was coming to New York in the near future, but I told Woollcott I'd be sure that he met the *Sanctuary* author if he paid a visit.

The large Woollcott following that had heard the *Sanctuary* broadcast must have been persuaded to buy the novel, for sales picked up considerably in bookstores. Sales also increased because the book had been banned in Boston, a stricture credited with making any book sell well.

Fame and notoriety now came to Bill. On the crest of the pro and con discussions of his next work, he went to New York to bask in his new success. Among the literati the rush was on to meet him.

By then my own career in the world of publishing had prospered at the American Play Company, and several first-rate authors had become clients. So life for me began to get into a real swing, and my style of living became fancier. I lunched almost daily in either the Rose Room at the Algonquin or at Twenty-One. I fear that I not only dropped names but also table-hopped. I was invited to the theater on opening nights and considered myself to be rather "in the know." My friends were amusing, creative, and amiable.

Bill made two visits—the first quite brief, when he came up from Charlottesville with Hal Smith and others, after attending the Southern Literary Festival.

The second visit, a quite long one, occurred two weeks later. He brought with him and introduced to me a man from the University of North Carolina to whom he had promised manuscripts to be published in an all-Faulkner issue of *Contempo*. The two came to the office. Not expecting Bill, I had made a luncheon engagement with Hayward and a client. Hayward and I were in the American Play Company waiting room when Bill arrived with his companion. Bill looked bereft when I said I could not lunch with them, and Hayward, to whom I had just introduced the two new arrivals, asked his secretary to go along with them, saying he'd treat them to lunch. "Take them to the Murray

Hill Hotel, " he said. To Bill he said, "I think you'll like it. Enjoy yourselves. By the way, Mr. Faulkner, I think *Sanctuary* is a honey, and maybe I can do something about selling it to the pictures. Come on, Ben; we'll be late." On the way to lunch Hayward questioned me further about Bill.

Later, Bill regretted having committed manuscripts to *Contempo*. He asked me to help him cancel the arrangement, but it was too late. The pieces eventually appeared in *Contempo*.

Bill soon moved into the Algonquin. I had suggested to him that he would be content there, and he was. He was befriended by Frank Case, that remarkable boniface who was continually and freshly beguiled by the many luminaries, greater and lesser, who frequented his hostelry and made of it a kind of clubhouse.

During one of his first days at the Algonquin, Bill had lunch with me there. He enjoyed watching the antics of a few of the famous, or infamous, Round Table habitués, those sometimes called the "Vicious Circle." He said he thought they were "showing off."

He had just completed a handwritten version of a short story. His handwriting, almost infinitesimal and illegible, was indecipherable to almost anyone unaccustomed to it. After lunch when we returned to his room, he could not find the manuscript. We made a thorough search and, failing to find it, went immediately to the lobby to report to Frank Case that it was missing.

Upstairs, the three of us made a second search, without success, then went to the basement and dug into garbage cans. No missing manuscript was uncovered. Frank, by this time, was practically in shock. In the lobby, he wiped his brow. "In all my years as manager I never had such a thing happen. I can't tell you, Mr. Faulkner, what this has done to me."

"Oh, Mr. Case," Bill said, looking up, his head cocked to one side, "if I wrote it once, I expect I can remember it and write it again." And then he invited Frank and me to his room for a highball. When he returned to Oxford, he did rewrite the story.

In his present success, Bill was in fairly easy financial circumstances. He told me of payments on Rowan Oak, improvements on the house, and doctor's bills for Estelle who had anemia, explaining that he was still pinched for money. But things definitely were better for him.

He often was parsimonious and squeezed pennies if not dollars, but he enjoyed good food and liquor and didn't stint himself on either. And at this time he very much needed diversion. He was still grieving over the loss of his and Estelle's first baby, Alabama. She had been named for one of his favorite aunts, and that fact had added to his pain. The story he told me about Alabama's birth and death appalled me.

Long afterward I learned that most of it he had, for some weird reason, almost wholly fabricated. He often manufactured tales about himself, and even now that makes it difficult to write about him and separate the "wheat of truth from the chaff of lies," to use a phrase I once heard him use, grinning when he said it. He relished exaggeration and what he called high flown speech. But I've strayed from the story he recounted of Alabama's death.

In those early days of his marriage he was sorely and continuously hard-pressed for money. He told me that sometimes his financial situation made him desperate. Estelle was fragile and ill much of the time. She was terribly thin, and she and Bill had been told that she wasn't physically up to bearing a child. Already she had borne Cornell Franklin two children, Victoria (or Cho-Cho) and Malcolm, and her health had been poor ever since. Despite the doctor's warning, Estelle became pregnant.

The baby was prematurely born. She was a puny, little thing, Bill said. All this he told me one night at the Algonquin, and there were tears in his eyes as he spoke. The doctor in attendance said that under no circumstances should Estelle or the infant be removed from the hospital.

Yet bills were mounting daily. Frantic and with the assistance of the family retainer, Mammy Callie, Bill took his wife and child to Rowan Oak, several miles from the hospital. He planned for Mammy Callie to attend Estelle and Alabama.

The health of both baby and mother worsened. At dawn one morning, Mammy Callie awakened Bill, who was sleeping in the next room. The first chirpings of birds could now be heard, and a faint dawn was vanishing the darkness from the sky—as Bill told the story. He said he followed the old black woman to the crib and looked at the baby, who was having difficulty breathing. He hurried to the phone downstairs to call the doctor who had delivered the baby. Bill told me that the doctor was brusque and that there was nothing he or anyone else could do and closed the conversation. Soon, with Mammy Callie and the young father watching, the child died. Estelle had not awakened. Bill said that he took a pistol from a bureau drawer and told the nurse to watch Estelle closely. He went to the circular driveway where the car was parked and drove to the doctor's house, crazed with grief. He called loudly to the doctor. When he stepped out on the front porch, Bill said he shot once, striking the doctor in the shoulder. He fell to the floor.

When Bill drove away, the doctor's wife and some neighbors rushed to help the wounded man. The wound was
superficial, and no charges were brought against Bill.

"The bastard deserved to die," Bill concluded his inven-
tion. People of the town sided with him, he added.

A true story? A fabrication? The latter I have come to
believe.

There was no doubt that by the time Bill arrived in New
York he had reached the status of a celebrity in the book
world. Of course, the man in the street or people who
might be sitting next to him in the subway or on a Fifth
Avenue bus had no idea who he was—just another smallish, stocky man whose nose was aquiline, whose eyes were
dark and piercing, and whose mouth was thin-lipped beneath a medium-sized moustache.

The Algonquin crowd and the one in Tony's Speakeasy
recognized him as the author of *Sanctuary*. Now and then
some in these places introduced themselves to him, and in
his soft voice Bill replied to questions and compliments.
He was feeling sweet success and what it meant to be
recognized as an outstanding writer.

One day as he and I were walking past Scribner's Book
Store on Fifth Avenue, we noted in the window a display of
biographies of a recently deceased author. "They'll be pick-
ing my bones one of these days," Bill said. "I'd better watch
what I do or say from now on, hadn't I?"

His clique of new friends gave him great pleasure—the
group I had introduced him to, in addition to others I
didn't know as well as he did.

Thinking back to those days, I still consider the apartment of Marc Connelly and his wife Madeline to have been
Bill's favorite place. There he enjoyed the company of

Frank Sullivan, Alice and Harold Guinzburg, Dorothy Parker, Russel Crouse, Alison Smith, Muriel King, and Allen Saalberg. Marc's wife had once been the Mack Sennett bathing beauty, Madeline Hurlock. Still beautiful, she was warm-hearted and generous, as was Marc, who was celebrated for the play *The Green Pastures* which he had so superbly adapted from Roark Bradford's stories, *Ol' Man Adam and His Chillun*. This couple extended gracious hospitality in their charming apartment in the Elysée Hotel. In spite of the apartment's luxury, there was a feeling of hominess.

Hearts was a favorite card game among this same group. It required no great skill or expertise, and Bill played it with zest. Word games did not appeal to him so much, but he took part in them. Puns were a favorite pastime, and the crowd took pleasure in very, very bad ones and found appeal in sheer outrageousness, but not in Bill's anemically inferior puns. I think he was somewhat upset that he wasn't more adroit.

Having listened to one of Bill's more feeble efforts at a pun, or to his constant repetition of "touché" when there was a scoring of friendly insult, Miss Dorothy, as Bill always addressed Mrs. Parker, drew me aside one night and, with her plaintive, endearing, hands-clasped-to-bosom gesture (Connelly once told her that she was as helpless and innocent as a black widow spider), murmured: "If dear Mr. Faulkner wouldn't try so hard to be funny. He should leave it to the likes of us to see how feather-brained we can be. My God, his wit is execrable. He's too great a man for our kind of foolishness. If he says 'touché' one more time in my presence, I'll let out a scream no one will call 'girlish!'" The others were more tolerant when he ventured to compete with them at "brain games," as he called them.

All in that crowd were drinkers except Crouse, who had

been a longtime teetotaler. None drank excessively. Bill was a moderate drinker when he was at the Elysée with the Connellys and others. There I never once knew him to go overboard. With them all was happiness and content- ment—the two emotional states which he most longed for and which thereafter he knew so seldom.

Lillian Hellman also lived at the Elysée in those days. Miss Hellman was a brilliant, high-minded person with enor- mous integrity and, despite a sometimes hard-boiled man- ner, a generous, warm woman. She and Bill liked each other. Dashiell Hammett, to me the greatest of all detec- tive writers, also liked Bill, and the three saw one another frequently. Bill didn't talk in detail with me about the time spent with other people, except for some vague mention now and then.

One night Hammett took Bill and me on a tour of some of the town's lesser known drinking haunts. Bill was eager to see the places owned and frequented by gangsters and the tough or lawless. One club I remember that night was called the Aquarium, decorated in a piscatorial theme. The bar was a glass aquarium, and from the top and sides one could look down at fish swimming about, among them large, expensive-looking goldfish. The proprietors also had selected Ye Olde panelings of dark wood and a massing together of tankards. Whatever the decoration, the liquor, though costly, was vile.

"They always tell you it comes over on a boat," Bill said. "The ferry boat from Hoboken I reckon's the boat they're talking about." He told me that he had done some rum running while he was in New Orleans or in Pascagoula, Mississippi. Again, true or false?

Dash Hammett was an excellent guide. He had much dignity and his sharp eyes and reserved manner were similar to Bill's. He had a keen sense of fun that appeared intermittently when least expected.

At one speakeasy that night, where the decor was early American, Hammett said, "The Pilgrim fathers had it pretty good with bars like this one," and Bill laughed. Then while Hammett and I got lost in a discussion, Bill wandered away, and I forgot about him. Then I saw him in earnest and absorbed conversation with a dark squatty man who was constantly gesticulating and raising his very dark eyebrows.

"That was a nice young fellow," Bill said, rejoining us. "Sort of a horticulturist. Grows roses, he says."

"No doubt," Hammett said. "His main interest, though, isn't roses. He's a king among rum runners and an all-around tough baby." Then he told us more about the notoriety of Bill's "nice" acquaintance.

Soon after, Bill returned to Oxford, and I sent him a gory account from a tabloid—*The Graphic*, probably—of the horticulturist's being gunned down in a gang war. Bill never mentioned the clipping. I laughed with Hammett about Bill and the gangster. "He called him 'nice,'" said Hammett. "I'd rather be cozy with a rattler."

Bill remained in New York for almost eight weeks. It was one of the happiest times in his life. If he was drinking too much, I never saw it. There was much time, though, that I wasn't with him when he roamed around with Jim Devine and other friends. He often spoke to me about Estelle and his worry about her health. And he was pleased in a modest way with his celebrity. In later years, he would wistfully recall incidents of the visit.

As I've pointed out, he loved theater, so I took him to several Broadway shows. I vividly remember his reactions to two of them—*The Front Page* and *Hamlet*. When I obtained tickets for *The Front Page*, I thought he would, like the critics, rave about it. In fact, he heartily disliked it, saying it was too noisy. "Entirely irresponsible theater," is the way he reported his feelings about it.

On the other hand, Norman Bel Geddes's production of *Hamlet*, a *succès d'estime*, found high favor with Bill. Bel Geddes's production introduced Raymond Massey to New York audiences and led to Massey's later huge following in motion pictures and television.

At intermission Bill didn't say a word but puffed away at his pipe, engrossed and reflective. I didn't interrupt his thoughts. As we left the theater he suddenly stopped. "Well, suh," he said in his soft, Deep South way, "I've just crossed over Jordan." And I knew that he had found *Hamlet* an exalting experience. As we walked on Broadway, he talked excitedly of several effects Geddes had introduced in his version, for example, the use of a roaming light to represent the ghost of Hamlet's father, with the speeches seeming disembodied.

"A good innovation," Bill called it, "giving an ethereal effect without being gruesome or morbid, but possessing overtones of sadness." He said that he would like to meet Bel Geddes.

I called the tireless and touched-with-genius Bel Geddes, who was one of my author clients and a good friend. He would be pleased to meet William Faulkner.

At first, they didn't hit it off very well. They were friendly, yes, but there was an emptiness in their conversation. Naturally, Bel Geddes liked Bill's comments about *Hamlet* and the producer's fine and fresh coloration. Bel Geddes spoke of *Sanctuary*, but Bill avoided the subject. Then I brought up Bel Geddes's "war game," a pastime he had devised, an amusement indulged in weekly by passionate players. It was elaborate, intricate, and as martially correct as war itself—both army and navy elements being called into play. We went upstairs where the war game was set up, left exactly as maneuvers were at the close of the last battle, or portion of battle. Bill was completely fascinated and asked numerous intelligent questions about different military techniques.

Then Bel Geddes, in a complete non sequitur, made some glib remark about *Sanctuary*. Bill froze. I wish I could recall what caused the tension. Hastily I asked Bel Geddes to bring out some of the magnificent masks he had created for a proposed production of Dante's *Inferno*. Bel Geddes quickly realized his error and brought out the masks.

Forgetting his pique, Bill delicately touched the masks, examining each one carefully, in admiration.

"O'Neill had the right idea in *The Great God Brown*," he said. "Those masks he used for his characters made a small play into a big one. But your masks are incredibly lovely; they express emotion in a way no human being could express it. Maybe that's the way all plays should be done."

He and Bel Geddes continued to talk about individual masks and their dramatic interpretation and possible impact on audiences. Bel Geddes was a fluent talker, and Bill could be a marvelous listener. By this time the two had become drawn to one another, and the only meeting they ever had came to a successful conclusion.

Dorothy Parker was living at the Algonquin, and her apartment was the meeting place for her cronies and also for freeloaders. One afternoon she invited Bill and me for a drink. As Bill was moving about companionably, a lively and quite pretty girl arrived on the arm of one of Dottie's current beaux. It was obvious that the uninvited girl was from the South. Her speech dripped with honeysuckle, and she addressed everyone as "Honey." She clung to the young man who had unwisely brought her to meet Mrs. Parker, who did not bother to ingratiate herself to the guest and continuously shot stiletto glances at the young man. He managed a quick exit, and when the door closed behind the pair, Dottie proceeded to make highly derogatory remarks about them. Among the less unkind things was a reference to "Little Missie Magnolia."

"Now, Mrs. Parker," Robert Benchley said, "I don't think that child would harm a fly."

Dottie raised her brown eagle-like eyes to him. "Not even an open fly?" she inquired.

"Touché," Bill said.

As Bill and I descended in the elevator, he said to me, "Miss Dorothy is a mighty tough lady, ain't she?" He was still talking colloquially in his dirt farmer role and not in that of the old Southern colonel or of the worldly literary figure, three roles he moved among depending on the occasion or his mood.

Frank Sullivan and Corey Ford, then two of New York's best and best-known humorists, shared an apartment on Beekman Place at East 51st Street, a few doors west of the apartment building where I was living. Bill liked both fellows and we went to see them frequently. He sometimes went without me and borrowed a typewriter. Their good Scottish housekeeper gave him the run of the apartment if they were out.

Corey had hired a professional decorator to do the apartment for him in what Sullivan called "very late collegiate." And it wasn't unlike fraternity living rooms, but it was a pleasant place to visit and was certainly a lively one. Bill thought Sullivan was a wry fellow, and Corey, seeming more solemn, he found to be filled with unexpected twists of quirkiness. Bill didn't wait for an invitation to go to their place, and they didn't object, because they liked him too.

Corey had written a parody of *Sanctuary*. His parodies, written under the pen name John Riddell, were first published in *Vanity Fair*, to which he was a regular contributor. The parodies, brought together as books by Scribner's, amused Bill, especially the one of *Sanctuary*. He considered it to be as good as Beerbohm's parody.

Late one afternoon, when we called, the housekeeper admitted us and told us that Sullivan and Ford were out. We looked at the books on the living room shelves, and Bill took out a copy of *Sanctuary*. He went to a table, and, noting that the book belonged to Ford, he wrote with his fountain pen, beneath Ford's signature of ownership, this, or similar sentiments: "To Frank Sullivan, this book, which belongs to Corey Ford." Corey was rather miffed, and we teased him about it. Sullivan, needless to say, was delighted.

"You know what I was saying when I wrote *Sanctuary*, don't you?" Bill had come into my office one day to write an introduction for the Modern Library edition of that book. I had, without difficulty, persuaded Bennett Cerf to include it in the Modern Library list of old and new classics or semiclassics.

Morty Goldman, then my assistant, came in, and I gave him the handwritten copy for him to type so that I could send it on to Bennett.

"I was saying that women are impervious to evil," Bill continued, as Morty closed the door.

"Not really?"

"Yes," he said. "You remember how Temple sat with her father, Judge Drake, in the Luxembourg Gardens? How she sat there on a bench, so quiet and so serene? And just as if none of those horrific things that happened to her in the old house and the corn crib or in the whorehouse with Pop Eye and her lover, Red, even occurred. She wasn't demoralized or touched by any of it. All of it was like water falling on a duck's back and sliding right off."

"What you say's tough on women."

"They'll survive."

Morty returned with the "Introduction" and handed it to Bill, who thanked him. As Morty started to leave again, Bill called to him and gave him the original holograph copy of the "Introduction," thanking him for favors he had done. Morty was deeply grateful. He later traded it to Bennett for several fine limited editions.

In this famous essay Bill created controversy by stating that he had written the book for the purpose of making money.

Passing the Metropolitan Opera House, Bill remarked that he'd never been in an opera house or seen a live opera anywhere. I remembered that one night at Ole Miss as Bill and I were listening to a record of *Carmen*, he had said, "Some of the music sounds as if it were composed for tin soldiers to march by."

I called Marise Hamilton, a friend who had the privilege of using an affluent kinsman's open box in the Diamond Horseshoe. For the night *Carmen* was scheduled she invited Bill and a few of her friends to join her. All of us were in evening rig ("full fig" as Bill described the attire) except Bill, the guest of honor. He wore slacks and a tweed jacket, white shirt and dark tie.

He didn't speak during the performance. He was recognized and nodded to during intermission while we were in the bar. When the opera ended, he thanked his hostess profusely and said good night to the other guests. Then we left to go to a beer party on upper Broadway. I asked Bill if he had enjoyed grand opera.

"It'd be mighty fine if they just wouldn't sing," he said.

The party we attended was something of a wake for a New York newspaper that was shutting down. Beer kegs were set around the room, and we immediately felt the usual spirit of conviviality. Among others who were not journalists we met Bing Crosby. Afterward, as we drove down Broadway, we passed the Paramount Theatre with a twinkling sign on its marquee, "Bing Crosby and His Band." Bill, observing the marquee, asked, "Was that the same little man I just met, Bing Crosby?"

I was trying to find employment for Bill writing motion picture scripts when Leland Hayward informed me that he had made an appointment for Bill with the East Coast representative of a Hollywood studio. "All your man has to do is be pleasant and we've got him a deal."

I accompanied Bill to the appointment, and the receptionist announced us. Bill followed me into the interviewer's office. He didn't rise from his chair behind a large and ornate desk but sat studying Bill. Finally, after the inspection he invited us to take chairs. He asked Bill why he wanted to write scripts.

"To make some money," Bill replied.

"That's telling me straight, isn't it?"

"You asked me straight. I answered you straight," Bill said and lit his pipe.

I was almost squirming in my chair. I realized Bill was riled and didn't care what he said at that point.

"What have you written worthwhile?"

"Mostly poems that I consider very worthwhile." Bill smoked his pipe placidly, seemingly oblivious of the representative's reddening face.

"Do you think you could be congenial with other writers at our studio?"

"Is it some kind of fraternity? Will I have to learn a secret password when I'm initiated?"

"No, it's not a club, but we do encourage amiable relationships among our employees."

"I can be amiable, but I thought I'd be paid for just writing."

It's too late for me to be saved, I thought.

"What actors and actresses do you especially like?"

"I don't especially like any of them since I hardly ever go to moving pictures at home. I do like the cartoons. I believe I could write some good cartoons. Scripts for 'em."

"We weren't thinking about cartoons," said the gentleman behind the desk. He seemed about to stand up. Then he sank back into his chair. I slumped. Bill sat erect, still puffing away at his meerschaum as the meeting rapidly grew more and more disastrous. Finally, the man was standing. "I believe that covers the major points. I'll telephone Hayward."

Needless to say, Bill didn't get the job. Hayward told me that the movie representative had asked him if "Faulkner is crazy, or just doesn't want to work for a studio."

I told Bill, and he said, "I reckon I'll have to do it sometime, but, by God, I'd sure hate to get in with a nut like the one we talked to. Maybe I'd better get off my high horse and act better next time I'm interviewed. I'm sorry I made such a mess about the job."

Later, of course, through Hayward, Bill was employed on the West Coast as a writer in the moving picture industry.

This ancient and hoary memory of mine—as Alexander

Woollcott might have called it—turns now to Woollcott himself.

Woollcott, whom Edna Ferber called the "New Jersey Nero," was not on his best behavior on the night Bill and I called on him at the Barclay Hotel. Having learned that Bill was in town, the Master had had his secretary telephone me to arrange the meeting with Faulkner that I had promised him. Bill said he didn't want to meet Woollcott, for the things he'd heard about him were not especially promising. I agreed, but I said that Woollcott could also be delightful and that he wielded considerable influence. His "Town Crier" broadcast on *Sanctuary* had been a good turn. So Bill decided he'd better see him.

Woollcott liked his followers to hover over him during the late night hours, so we set a time after the theater. When we arrived, we were invited into the apartment by one of Woollcott's favorites of the moment. Bill and I were shown into the living room, where a large gathering surrounded our host. He lounged against pillows on a sofa. He was garbed in a rather tattered red brocade dressing gown, the sash untied. His fat belly protruded where the pajama top was not buttoned.

Ah," he said, arms extended, his head tilted upward in an overalert, inquisitive manner. "So, it's Master Faulkner, not looking in the least bit sinister. I observe you don't have your corncob with you." Bill remained silent, as Woollcott looked about to see if those in the room understood the allusion.

He turned his attention to me. "And here's Washington." This was what he jokingly called me now and then. "By the way, Washington, I've frequently intended to ask you an important and personal question."

"Yes?" I said, waiting for a derogatory jibe.

"How much Negro blood do you have?" He felt certain the inquiry would insult me.

"Half," I said.

His mouth dropped in chagrin. "I wondered, not that it's in the least relative to anything important."

He turned to Bill and was abeam again. "You disappoint me, young Massa. You seem much too harmless to have written that horror of a book. Now, tell me, is Missy Temple a typical Southern belle?".

For a moment Bill hesitated. Then he turned around and moved toward the door through which we had entered. From the elevator I followed him to the street. Outside, he stopped so abruptly that I almost ran into him.

"I'd prefer to keep company with Frankenstein's monster," he said.

Bennett Cerf was delighted when I told him Bill wanted to visit Harlem. Bennett told Carl Van Vechten, who offered to accompany us there. Van Vechten was a true aficionado of that neighborhood, which had been "taken up" as a chic place by certain white people.

Bennett invited Bill, Tiah Devitt, author of *The Aspirin Age*, and me to dine at his apartment with his father, Van Vechten, and himself. He also invited Alfred Knopf.

As soon as Bill entered Bennett's living room overlooking Central Park, he went to the windows, remarking that the view was superb at night and that the city was fortunate to have a park with so many trees. He praised the magical effect of flashing car headlights in the park.

The dinner was most pleasant. Knopf was engaging, and Bennett, with his infectious laughter, added a spontaneous amiability. Van Vechten regaled us with accounts of Harlem folkways, arts, and the overall attractiveness of the district.

Bill told Miss Devitt that she reminded him of *The Young Salome* in the Metropolitan Museum of Art. Miss Devitt, he declared, had the same gypsy quality and the painter's suggestion of the sinister. I think Miss Devitt was pleased by the comparison.

At that time Knopf, Bennett, and Harold Guinzburg were wooing Bill in the hope that if he departed from Hal Smith one of them could acquire him as an author. It had been rumored that Smith's firm was in financial trouble.

Following dinner, as Bennett was serving coffee and liqueurs, Knopf went into the foyer and returned shortly with several books. Extending them to Bill he said, "Mr. Faulkner, I brought along your books. I'd appreciate it if you'd autograph them for me."

"I only autograph my books to my close friends," Bill replied courteously, "but I appreciate the compliment you pay in asking me."

Knopf, obviously taken aback, left the room.

Afterwards as we were leaving the apartment, Bill went to the foyer and returned to the living room with the books. "I signed them, Mr. Knopf, and broke my rule about autographing because you have been such a good friend to books and authors during your publishing career, and because of the good taste your house has brought to publishing." Bill made a courtly bow and handed the books to Knopf.

On the way uptown Van Vechten continued to talk of Harlem to Miss Devitt and me. He said that Harlemites were the happiest folk in America, a statement which doubtless would meet with disagreement. "It's a new world for creative people," he said. "Negroes possess from birth a rare talent for bringing their special heritage to the arts. They have brought about a renaissance with their unique sensory and dusky quality."

"Sorry, Mr. Vechten, I don't think you'd find much of that in the South," Bill said.

"They haven't had a chance."

"You don't need a chance to create. You just do it."

The taxi stopped before a small brick building, and Van Vechten, after paying the taxi driver, gestured us to the sidewalk. At the grille door he rang a bell and was immediately recognized and invited in. We were led through a small room crowded with tables and people, both black and white. The room was filled with smoke that obscured things, and the odor of gin and whiskey was strong. We were seated at a table for four almost in the center of the room. The piano and singing were loud and shut off conversation.

In the middle of the room Gladys was singing one of her more popular and vulgar numbers. Gladys's Place was one of the best liked of the Harlem nightspots. I believe she composed many of her songs herself. They were filled with double entendres, but the obscenities were supposedly subtle. She rolled her eyes and whirled her body about as she performed. She dressed in a tuxedo and worked as hard as a field hand at her act. Swaying and clapping her hands, she was a sight to behold. Her body never stopped its lewd motion.

"Look how she's ogling me," Tiah said.

"Obviously she thinks you're pretty," said Van Vechten.

Sitting stiffly, Bill said nothing. The skinny black man at the piano who accompanied Gladys was beaming, his face dripping sweat. Gladys came to the end of the many verses of "Sweet Violets," and the customers screamed and yelled and applauded.

Bill got up from the table. "Mr. Van Vechten, you've been instructive, and I appreciate your kindness, but I'm tired. New York isn't an easy town for such a country man as I am, so I'll say good night." He took Tiah by an elbow. Van Vechten protested that the evening had just gotten underway and there were other clubs he wanted to take us to. Bill thanked him again. I followed Tiah and Bill out.

"Now I've seen Harlem," he said, hailing a cab.

In the cab he said, "Down in Memphis, I wouldn't spend my time on Beale Street mixing around socially, and I wouldn't do it again in New York's Harlem. It's a fad to do it and sensation-seeking."

"I have a good time when I go," Tiah said.

"A nice, pretty young lady like you hasn't any business in dumps like that."

Helen Grace Carlisle, whose first novel *See How They Run* had been published by Cape and Smith, met Bill and invited him and me to a cocktail party. She was a small, pretty young woman whose lifestyle was objectionable to strict moralists. She was researching a second book dealing with the early days of American Puritans—studying their customs, clothes, speech, and so forth. During one afternoon in Brooklyn she had talked at great length about her efforts to keep her facts completely correct. She had drawn Bill away from other guests and was in earnest conversation with him. On the subway back to Manhattan, I asked Bill what they had talked about.

He said it was about her research, laughing. "It wasn't exactly what you'd call a conversation," he said. "A conversation's when two or more folks talk. When it's just one, I believe it's a monologue. Who cares exactly how they ate, talked, or fornicated?" he said. "The main thing I told the young lady is to give an effect of veracity. She wanted to know what I do about 'researching' Indians. I told her I don't. Long as they don't say 'Ugh' or 'How' I think I make 'em real." He grinned at me, and for a moment I thought he looked like a 'possum.

It was one of the most beautiful rooms I had ever been in. As I think I remember it was decorated in various shades of blue. Two windows overlooked the East River which was quietly lovely, gleaming softly in the subdued glow of lights of boats and barges reflecting in the water.

This was in the apartment of Adele and Robert Lovett, who had invited guests there for an evening. "All very informal," she had said. The guest list included people Bill had met in New York, but also people neither he nor I had met. Adele Lovett had a bewitching soft quality, and whenever I saw her she was wearing blue. Women cattily said that she was always working on a piece of blue needle-point.

Robert Lovett was a gregarious host. He came up to Bill, and they got into talk about World War I, and Bill told him, incorrectly, that he had served with the RAF as a "leften-ant."

Lovett plunged into a story about an experience he had had in England during the war. In a seaside town he had often noticed young British servicemen attached to His Majesty's Navy lying about the street near the docks in various stages of drunkenness. There they lay, their dirty uniforms in disarray. He learned that they engaged in in-credibly dangerous sorties in torpedo boats against enemy ships. They made bets with each other on hits, near hits, and misses. "They were lads who probably had just begun to shave," Lovett said sadly. "It was the goddamnedest thing I ever heard of."

Bill asked him to describe again the boats and torpedoes, and Lovett did, though he quickly changed the subject.

On the way back to the Algonquin—a long walk—Bill didn't say a word directly to me, but he muttered to himself over and over such remarks as, "Those pore young sons of bitches. Just beginning to live. No wonder they stayed drunk."

At the Algonquin he pleaded with me, though it was very late, to go with him to his room and join him in another drink. I did as he wished, but I made a move to leave after we had a highball. He had scarcely spoken a word.

"Please don't leave me. Spend the night here, Ben. I can't stand to be alone tonight." I gave him another drink, then lay back on his bed and went to sleep almost immediately.

From Oxford not much later on he sent me a new short story. It had been expanded, but basically it was Lovett's account, with fine fictional inventions. I sold it to the *Saturday Evening Post*, which published it as "Turn About." Within a fairly short time Leland sold it to Metro-Goldwyn-Mayer, and it was made into a motion picture starring Franchot Tone, Clark Gable, and Joan Crawford. There had been no female in Bill's short story, and when he saw the motion picture version Bill was said to have remarked: "Maybe Joan Crawford was a more deadly threat to those boys than those torpedoes would ever be."

While he had been nearing the end of that New York visit, Bill had asked me what I thought of his writing Estelle to join him for a visit there. "She's had such a tough time lately, what with the baby dying and poor health. I'd like to get her mind off bad things." I answered that it should be fine and we'd make plans to give her a good time.

She accepted and would soon arrive on the Southerner, a popular train that ran between New Orleans and New

York. When Bill finally determined to do something, he went about it at once. He planned a party in Estelle's honor. I helped him with a list of people to whom he was obligated, and we went to Frank Case and told him to make all the arrangements for a certain night and time—food, drinks, flowers—in one of the private rooms at the Algonquin. We felt in secure hands with Frank taking charge.

Bill, Harold Guinzburg, and I were at the Pennsylvania Station to meet Estelle. She seemed exhausted, and her eyes were enormous in her thin face, but she was making every effort to be animated and was even a bit kittenish. On the way to the hotel she chattered constantly. I had not seen Bill and Estelle together since their marriage, and I noticed that he covertly watched every move she made and that her sidelong glances at him in the cab seemed to me to be questioning.

She was most cordially received in New York the few days she was there. Everyone who had been invited to her party came, and a few who had not been invited also came.

Among the guests were Hal and Clare Spencer, Maurice Hindus, Tiah Devitt, Frank Sullivan, Marc and Madeline Connelly, Dorothy Parker, Harold and Alice Guinzburg, Muriel King, and Bennett Cerf, with whom Estelle danced and flirted.

Woollcott, who had not been invited, made a conspicuous entrance. He soon departed after Bill was plainly abrupt with him. That was the only sour note in the otherwise happy evening.

During the party Bill came to me now and then. "Estelle's not drinking too much, is she?" She wasn't. Or Estelle would whisper to me: "Don't let Billy drink too much." He didn't.

From Oxford I soon received from Estelle and Bill a beautiful dressing gown, accompanied by a gracious note thanking me for helping make their "stay in New York a wonderful one."

Before long Bill sent me a manuscript of a novel by Estelle. It was overwritten and melodramatic. He asked me to do whatever I could with it because she was "driving me crazy" to help her get it published. I returned the manuscript with a friendly note, telling Bill that I was going to California—Hollywood—to see what I could find in those hills and suggested that he let Morton Goldman handle his work since he was entirely capable. Bill accepted the idea.

The market crash had hurt the publishing business. That was one of the reasons I went to Hollywood.

I was to encounter Bill there, too. But it was quite different being with him in that odd city, different from Oxford, Greenville, or New York, and certainly not as satisfactory from many standpoints.

Hollywood

In Los Angeles and its environs, including Hollywood, I found the neighborliness of New York City entirely missing. Everything seemed spread all over the West Coast. In comparison, Manhattan wore an air of snugness; even with all its five boroughs, an intimacy of sorts then existed there. From the day I arrived riding on the train through sweet-smelling orange groves, I had the feeling that all the people I encountered were transients.

Jean Negulesco, a young Rumanian painter who was in the art department of Paramount Studios, had a house in Santa Monica, and he kindly invited me to share it with him until I found a place of my own. The invitation was extended with such warmth that I quickly accepted.

Negulesco was a top man in the art department. His own fine paintings hung throughout his house, which had a casual charm and showed his good taste. Paramount Studios had produced *The Story of Temple Drake* adapted from *Sanctuary*. Miriam Hopkins, who played the title role, was a friend of both Negulesco and me, and Leland Hayward had negotiated the motion picture sale of the book through the American Play Company.

In preparing art work for the picture, Negulesco had drafted a special group of black and white drawings, his own conception of the notorious rape scene. The drawings were stunning creations, giving suggestions of how the cameras should shoot the scene through Popeye's legs as he approached Temple Drake lying in the corn crib.

Bill was in Hollywood and I wanted him and Negulesco to meet, so Bill came to dinner one night. After we had eaten, the host showed him the portfolio of drawings. "Exactly what I had in mind," Bill praised, carefully studying the pictures. With an old-world charm of which he had more than his share, Negulesco gave Bill the album.

Because Bill had not seen the motion picture version of *Sanctuary* Negulesco asked him to come to Paramount for a private screening. Bill and I went together to see it. As the film progressed from reel to reel, he didn't speak, but when the showing was ended and the lights came on, he said that he had admired a great deal of the film. "Ruby is grand," he said of Florence Eldridge's role. He thought Miriam Hopkins as Temple was fine, adding, "I like the way she moves, seeming to dart, and she smells of femininity, woman, an aura of sex." He did not care especially for the others, with the exception of Miss Reba, who he said was "just grand."

As we left the studio he said, "Tell Negulesco I thank him for helping make the story into a moving picture I'm not ashamed of."

A Hollywood friend soon found me a small and rather quaint two-story house on Sweetzer down the street a block or so from Sunset Towers. The house I rented was one of four tiny "Alpine" chateaus, set in an attractively planted court. A New Yorker lived in the house across from mine, and together we employed one houseboy, a friendly, shy Philipino, Paul Pagurayan. The court and the houses reminded one of something belonging to Hansel and Gretel, but not so whimsical as to be sickening. I lived here until 1937.

My own bedroom upstairs was large, and adjoining it was a second room in which there were a couch and desk, with a bathroom conveniently situated to both rooms. Downstairs was a somewhat split-level living-dining room with kitchen connected.

It was at the small desk upstairs that Bill typed much of *Absalom, Absalom!* He typed, as was his custom, from his handwritten first draft. He would discard unsatisfactorily typed pages in a wastebasket to one side of the desk. As he pecked away with two fingers, he usually had the stem of his pipe clenched tightly between his teeth, making his mouth seem even smaller and thinner.

Sometimes he'd come downstairs where I was reading. "It's a tortured story," he said once, "and a torture to write it." Another time he said, "One thing I've learned to do right—get the right name for my people. I'm damn good at that. I might fail in other respects, but, yes, I always get the right name for my people." On another occasion, years later, he chuckled and said, "Somebody said I was a genius writer. The only thing I'd claim genius for is thinking up that name *Snopes*." I agreed with him wholeheartedly.

The first time Paul started emptying Bill's wastebasket he asked if it would be all right if he incinerated Bill's discards. Bill's response was, "Oh, hell, I don't care what he does with them. They sure ain't any good to me anymore. Why in hell would anybody want to save old typewritten pages? Handwritten ones, maybe." So they were disposed of by fire.

One afternoon when he was through with his typing for the time being, he came downstairs and sat beside me on the couch. I laid my book aside and, for a change, he lit a cigarette instead of a pipe.

"These damn cigarettes. Why in hell anybody smokes 'em I can't understand when a relaxing pipe's available. What were you reading? I can't seem to read anything but mysteries and detective stories." He picked up my book.

"Oh, Proust. *Swann's Way*. Swann! That pore misguided son of a bitch, and they call him a snob. I think he was just the opposite. Godamighty, what Odette did to him. To have crucified him would have brought him less hell, less anguish. In some ways Proust was lucky. He didn't ever have to contend with Hollywood for his bread and butter. I'd rather have spent my time in that corklined bedroom of his, asthma and all. Anytime."

He frequently griped about Hollywood but admitted that he had to have the money he made writing there. When I asked him how *Absalom* was progressing, he said, "It moves along. Word by word, sentence by sentence, page by page, and then one day a book's finished. Ain't any book easy to write," he added. "Lots simpler to make a coffin.

"This is a good house to work in," he said, looking around the small white-walled room, a clump of tall red poinsettias showing at one of the windows. "Look at those poinsettias. It's Christmas all year around out here. Santa Claus must get confused. I know I do."

Associated as we were with different talent agencies, I didn't see Bill a lot in Hollywood. Socially, I mingled with people he didn't care for. I had invited him several times to go to one or another of the parties I was attending, but he politely refused the invitations. He had enjoyed being with people in New York and being gregarious. Hollywood, he declared, was different. There was something genuine about New York gatherings that he felt wasn't present in Hollywood. In fairness to Hollywood socializing, Bill didn't give it a real chance, and I did not urge him to do so.

One afternoon at my house, when he had finished typing, he said he'd like some Southern food for a change. So many fruit salads, he moaned. And hamburgers: "They'd put strawberries and whipped cream in 'em, if they

thought about it." He admitted that the fish dishes were
good, but he took no delight in abalone. "Abalone soup!" he
said scornfully.

Two friends, Dan Totheroh and George O'Neil, both
well-known playwrights, had a black woman cooking for
them, and upon hearing of Bill's wish, they asked us to
dinner. We accepted, and we took along Maurice Coindreau, who was visiting Bill. Coindreau was and still is, I
suppose, a superb translator of Bill's work into French.
"Early burlesque" is what O'Neil called their house. It
wasn't quite that bad, and the evening spent there was a
delightful one. Bill was sticking to milk or coffee and so I
was not worried that he would get drunk.

Coindreau proved to be amiable, with sparkling Gallic
charm. I knew that George and Dan liked him immediately
but were reserving their judgment about Bill, studying him
in a rather puzzled way.

Conversation remained lively. George was witty as he
usually was, and Dan laughed heartily. Bill, who had now
accepted some wine, complimented the hosts, then held
forth on the subject of wines in general. He wasn't actually
an oenophile, but he fancied that he knew a great deal
about the subject. I felt sure that Coindreau had a thorough
knowledge of wines and their vintages, but he listened to
Bill respectfully as Bill, sipping from his glass, expounded
pontifically. Fortunately, he drank sparingly and barely
sipped the after-dinner liqueur.

The dinner was good, well-prepared fried chicken, rice,
gravy, mustard greens, hot biscuits, and peach pie. Bill
enjoyed it thoroughly, and filled with food he liked and
good fellowship he treasured, he entered into the after-
dinner conversation. In an unheated argument about the
so-called great books, Bill said as far as he was concerned
Madame Bovary was his choice. He conceded, however,

that Balzac was a "bigger" (you could almost see the quotation marks as he said it) author than Flaubert. "*War and Peace* is too long," he said. "And Dostoyevsky gets tedious." He didn't make these judgments in a smug way. He spoke in praise of *Tom Sawyer* and felt that *Moby Dick* was this country's finest literature.

Coindreau said, bowing toward its creator, "*The Sound and the Fury* is in top place in your country." Bill replied, "*Merci, merci, Monsieur Coindreau, mon ami.*" That was the only French spoken during the evening.

The conversation lasted until after twelve o'clock. Bill said that if the cook hadn't gone home, he'd like to compliment her on the dinner. It happened that she lived in the house, and she came to the living room. "I can always tell when a cook comes from Mississippi," Bill said to her.

"Yes, sir, and thank you, but I was born in Alabama," she laughed.

"You're a neighbor anyhow, so I was close enough."

Nunnally Johnson was a producer, with David Hempstead his assistant, when Bill was working on a script for them at 20th Century Fox. The three men liked one another. Bill considered Nunnally a "character" and Dave a "good guy." He was pleased to be working on a script with producers he liked and respected and who didn't feel that the heavens would tumble down if a motion picture script didn't result in a money-making production. Neither Nunnally nor Dave was unctuous about the production of motion pictures, and Nunnally sometimes was ribald and irreverent about them. This attitude delighted Bill. He repeated to me various amusing things Nunnally had said to him.

Despite his seeming contentment, however, something triggered Bill's drinking. Dave telephoned me and said he feared that Bill was on the verge of trouble and asked if I would come to the studio and persuade Bill to return to the Beverly Hills Hotel where he was staying. I got to the studio as soon as I could and obtained a pass to visit Nunnally's quarters. I knew of the ironclad rule that anyone caught drinking at the studio would be immediately fired. Bill was sitting in his office, lackadaisically typing. He didn't look up as Dave and I stood inside the doorway, talking.

"Ben's come to see you," Dave said. "He was at the studio on business and thought he'd look in and say 'hello.'"

"He's come to see if I'm drinking," Bill said, without looking up.

"I've seen you drinking before," I said, rather angrily. "Remember Ole Miss? Remember New York?"

"Sure I remember. And I wish to God I was in either one of them. Excuse me, I've got to get this job finished, Bud." When he added the "Bud" I thought he might not be too hard to handle.

"Bill was tired," Dave said, "and it's quitting time, so I thought we might go to his hotel and get us a drink. Come on, Bill, since you don't have a car, I'll take you."

I followed them in my car, and when I arrived at Bill's hotel both he and Dave already had highballs in their hands.

"What kept you so long?" Bill asked.

"Traffic worse than usual," I told him.

Bill persuaded me to have a drink with them. In the short time I was in the room, his mood changed chameleonlike from semipleasant to belligerent.

"You're spying on me," he said. "I can tell. You want to tell Estelle. Go ahead. I don't give a damn what you tell her. So call her up. I reckon you'll find her in Oxford. So go ahead and do it."

I didn't attempt to argue with him. Dave remained quiet. As Bill finished his drink, his glass fell to the floor.

"I'm sleepy," he said. He lay down and almost instantly fell asleep. This was the first time I had seen him so completely drunk and so unpleasant. I hoped he would sleep all night and wake the next morning without needing a drink. Dave and I lowered the shades because the bright sunset was streaming across the bed. We left the room, sighing our relief. Dave telephoned the next morning to report that Bill came to the office early and seemed all right, rather sheepish, but not apologizing.

The so-called glamour crowd in Hollywood circles during the early thirties gave the already fabulous town its greatest glitter. Movie queens were just that, and movie kings were read about and worshiped. New and younger actors gleamed brightly, but it was stars such as Garbo, Swanson, Gable, and March, to name only a quartet of them, who shone brightest in the movie town's firmament. These are fancy words, maybe, but no fancier or more artificial than the period and its people.

None of this was of the slightest interest to Bill, and he made no effort to meet any of the high and mighty. He was the last person in the world who would have dreamed of getting on a sightseeing bus to have the "homes of the stars" pointed out to him, with tidbits monotonously narrated about the lives and doings of the occupants of the large houses. I never saw him wandering through the back lots of studios to see the sets: the streets, the houses, the buildings, western towns, eastern towns, southern and northern towns, all with false fronts.

But when I told him that Claudette Colbert, the beautiful French-born actress who was a friend of mine, had expressed a keen desire to meet him, he seemed rather pleased, and we set up a date to go to her house one afternoon. He said that he had seen *It Happened One Night* and admired her work in it and her famous legs.

We went to Miss Colbert's new house where she lived with her husband, Dr. Joel Pressman, and her mother, Madame Chauchoin, with whom I first had eaten snails, which she had prepared for several of us one night.

I introduced Bill to Miss Colbert, and she led us into the drawing room. She had begun to acquire some splendid paintings, and she guided him around the room proudly telling him about them and how and where she had purchased them. Most of them, I recall, were of the French Impressionist school. I have heard that she later became a talented painter whose works were praised by art authorities.

We sat for a while, she talking about her early life in France, telling Bill that her real name was Lily Chauchoin and that she didn't know exactly why she had chosen her professional name. He addressed her throughout the afternoon as "Miss Claudette" in the way some Southern men addressed all ladies, perhaps as a form of flattery.

He talked of Oxford and of his farm. For almost the entire visit, he assumed his dirt farmer role. He said he liked to paint, especially watercolors, but regretted that he didn't have much time to enjoy the hobby.

She asked if he'd like something to drink. "Yes, ma'am," he said, "if it wouldn't be too much trouble, I'd like a glass of sweet milk."

Miss Colbert looked at me and raised her handsome eyebrows. I knew she was puzzled and I explained, "Just

Ben Wasson and Claudette Colbert

plain milk." "Oh," she said, and left us. Bill roamed about the room, studying the paintings, admiring one espe-cially—perhaps it was a Utrillo, but I'm not certain.

She returned, followed by a maid with a tray with Bill's order and Coca-Cola for her and for me.

"My husband and I admire your books very much," Miss Colbert said.

"Thank you, ma'am. And I liked you in that picture with Clark Gable. I've met him."

"Clark's a great guy, and no foolishness about him. Fine to work with, too. Not temperamental at all."

"I don't know the movie stars, just writers that write the movies for the actors' and actresses' benefit."

The conversation began to drag, and I could see that Bill was becoming restless.

"My neighbor is ZaSu Pitts," she said. "Perhaps you've seen her in pictures, Mr. Faulkner?"

"Yes ma'am," he said. "I know she's a famous comedi-enne, but I saw her in a silent picture, *Greed*, a long time ago and she was fine in a serious part."

"Indeed she was," Miss Colbert said, "but playing those funny roles finally caught up with her, and nobody will cast her in a serious part for fear the audience might laugh at her." She rose from her chair. "I've told her you were coming this afternoon, and she thought you might enjoy a game of tennis. She has a fine court."

Bill got up and said that he'd be delighted to play a few sets, and we crossed over to Miss Pitts's adjoining prop-erty. She was at the front door when we got there. Miss Colbert introduced Bill to her. I already knew her, and we muttered the usual friendly amenities.

"I love to read, but I'm not a very literary person," Miss Pitts said to Bill as we strolled back to the court.

"Thank God for that," Bill said. "Not long ago I was

caught at a 'Literary Festival,' or whatever they called it, in Charlottesville, Virginia, and may the gods preserve me from another such."

Once on the tennis court it was decided that Bill and Miss Pitts would play singles while Claudette and I sat on the sidelines. It was an oddly matched game. Although both played fair enough tennis, one couldn't be very serious watching the players, because if she missed a ball or misplayed, she would cry out, "Oh, my," or "Oh, dear," sounding exactly as she did when she uttered the same words on the screen.

After their game, Miss Pitts, a teetotaler, invited us to have a soft drink but we declined. I wished she had offered us some of the home-made candy for which she became famous. Many years later she wrote a recipe book, *Candy Hits with ZaSu Pitts*.

It had been a pleasant afternoon with two stars, all homey, casual, and congenial. As we drove toward my house in Bill's car, he said, "Miss Claudette's legs are prettier when you really see them than they are on a movie screen, ain't they?"

I agreed that he was eminently correct.

Just as the Moslem faithful make their pilgrimage to Mecca, so the transient authors in Hollywood made their way to Stanley Rose's book shop. It was a haven from the boredom and stupidity of the motion picture capital. The shop was unpretentious. There was no effort to make it stylish. It was a *book* store. From under the counter Stanley Rose would, if he knew you well enough, produce a book of pornography. He was friendly and enthusiastic, and his hobby was living authors. He was a soft touch for any writer short of money, and I doubt that he ever dunned anyone for payment of an overdue account.

Bill met fellow craftsmen at Rose's such as John O'Hara and Budd Schulberg. He encountered Hammett there, and they resumed the friendship begun in New York. It was there he met the brilliant writer Nathanael West.

I went only one time with Bill to the Rose book store, though I went there at other times alone. Bill introduced me to Nathanael West, who told us that afternoon about hunting wild pigs on an island not far from Hollywood. He described what a magnificent, thrilling, and sometimes dangerous sport it was, and Bill was fascinated. Before we left the store, Bill had accepted an invitation to go on the next pig hunt. The two did hunt together, and I heard contradictory stories about the adventure. Some said that Bill got very drunk and was accidentally wounded. Other versions were that he behaved splendidly.

Is Stanley Rose's book shop still in Los Angeles? I don't know. I do know, though, that it was a place of revelation and solace to many authors and we'll not see again the like of its proprietor.

Late one night I was awakened by a telephone call from Bill. His voice, as usual, was soft and gentle, but I detected trouble in his tone. "I want to take you somewhere tomorrow to meet someone. Think you can go if I pick you up at your house? Late afternoon all right?"

I told him to come for me about 4:30. When he arrived and I got in his car, he said, "I'm glad you could go."

For several days there had been torrential rains and the streets were still flooded. "Funny thing about these rains and the hills out here," he said after we had ridden along for a while. He laughed softly. "Someone, maybe it was Nunnally—now ain't he a case?—said that when the hard rains come out here the Hollywood Hills all get washed away, but then they're putting them right back where they

belong the next day!" He lapsed into silence. His silences, I
had noticed, were more frequent and were lasting longer.
Some people were annoyed when he fell into one of these
long, impenetrable spells. I never felt—with one appalling
exception—a sense of embarrassment when he remained
silent. He said people "yapped" too much, anyhow.

I commented, "I believe all the derogatory remarks
made about Hollywood are made by foreigners like you and
me and everybody else who comes to get some of the fools'
gold. I doubt that a native son would make a slurring remark about it."

"I never met a native son. Rare as a native New Yorker.
Put 'em in a zoo," he said.

We talked of home and friends; then he switched the
subject suddenly. "We're going to Howard Hawks's house.
Ever meet him?"

I told him I had met him in New York once.

"A grand guy, one of the most decent to work for. No
front to Hawks."

"That's his reputation with everyone who knows him and
works with him," I agreed.

In Beverly Hills he turned the car into a driveway that
led through spacious grounds to a spacious house. Hawks
was waiting for us. "Hawks and I have some work to do,"
Bill said. "You don't mind waiting, do you?" I told him I
didn't mind, and we got out of the car. I reminded Hawks
when and where we had met, and he politely said he remembered the meeting. "Bill probably told you we have
some work to do. Rather come inside the house or wait out
here?"

I elected to sit on the patio, and he offered to have a
drink sent out, which I declined. So he waved a hand to the
tables piled with magazines. "Cigarettes in the boxes. Help
yourself," he said, and he and Bill left me.

Howard Hawks

What the hell? I thought. Then I had a hunch. Bill wanted me to meet a woman.

I was correct, for, in about half an hour, he and Hawks returned. With them was a tall, very good-looking young woman.

"This is Meta," Bill said.

She came forward and held out a hand. "Ben, I know you are such a good friend of Bill's. He's talked so much about you I feel as if I already know you." Her handclasp was firm.

I hadn't the remotest idea what her last name was, but I acknowledged the introduction and muttered something polite.

"Let's have a drink," Hawks said. I refused, as did Bill, who began to say good-bye and we soon departed. As Bill and I drove away, he said, his face straight ahead, "That is the girl I'm in love with. Can't get her out of my mind or system. And don't want to. You don't know what a wonderful person she is."

"She's certainly attractive," I said.

"She was brought up in Mississippi," he said, as if that explained everything, and I couldn't help smiling.

As we drove along he continued to tell me about her. This was the first time he had ever talked to me about someone with whom he was in love, with the exception of

Meta Carpenter

Helen Baird. He had never talked to me about being in love with Estelle, though of course I had heard many stories about their stormy romance and marriage, the subject of so much talk and speculation at the time in Oxford.

"She's brought me peace of mind. I haven't said anything yet to Estelle, who's already suspicious, I think. I want to marry Meta."

There was nothing I could say and we went on to my house. "I'll be calling you," he said and drove off.

Several Sundays afterward I went to a luncheon at Marc
Connelly's house. He and beautiful Madeline had di-
vorced, and he was on a writing job at a studio. I had seen
him several times, and once we had double-dated and
spent an evening dancing at the Ambassador. Soon after I
arrived at Marc's and joined a group in the garden, Bill and
Meta came in together. They were taken around by Marc
and introduced. Dorothy Parker was there, and she and
Bill greeted each other affectionately.

Socially, I noticed, Meta was wholly at ease, talking
animatedly with the guests. Marc, with considerable
amusement, was showing everyone a "hangover remedy"
which he professed to believe had great financial promise.
The medicine was wrapped, as I recall, in some kind of red,
white, and blue paper.

"These colors," Mrs. Parker exclaimed, examining the
kit, "are worse than a hangover. But I'll try it and be a
guinea pig now since I was a plain pig last night. My God,
will I ever learn anything!"

Later, Estelle, their three- or four-year-old child Jill, and a
black nurse and driver arrived in Hollywood. Bill had telephoned me and told me his family was headed west for a
visit with him. He groaned. I said I would be glad to see
Estelle again and was eager to know Jill. He doted on her
and talked of her often. Soon after their arrival, I was invited to their house for dinner. Bill had told Estelle that I
was dating Meta, and he asked me if I minded bringing
her. A young man named Jerry who was in the Selznick
office was to pick us up. Bill went on to say that I was
supposed to be Meta's beau. He wanted Meta to meet
Estelle, and this was the only arrangement he could think
of without arousing Estelle's suspicion. I thought it was a
terrible idea, and I felt a sense of betrayal, but I agreed to

Meta Carpenter, William Faulkner, Ben Wasson, and Dorothy
Parker at Marc Connelly's house

Marc Connelly, Ben Wasson, and William Faulkner at
Connelly's house

his unpalatable scheme. "But be careful," he had warned. "Estelle'll catch on if you're not careful."

When Meta, Jerry, and I got to Bill's rented residence, both he and Estelle came to the door to meet us and ushered us into a not very attractive living room. It was a rented house, and Estelle, who had much talent for making a house charming, had had no opportunity to decorate. She and Meta, when I introduced them, gave one another that femininely characteristic once-over, and I was reminded of Bill's comment so many years before that even small girls, when they meet for the first time, looked one another over, and knew everything about each other.

After a bit of polite chatter on the part of everyone except Bill—he puffed away at his pipe—Estelle said she'd bring us drinks and hors d'oeuvres. Jerry, Bill, and I, with Meta making a comment now and then, talked about Hollywood personalities, mostly the writers we all knew. Estelle returned with a tray of glasses and a pitcher that held what looked like martinis. I thought, "Hold your hats, boys, here we go again!"

"You're not drinking, are you Billy?"

"I guess not if that's what you've decided for me."

The rest of us poured from the pitcher and lifted our glasses in a half-hearted toast.

"To Hollywood," Estelle said. She was twitching nervously.

"No, to Mississippi," Meta said.

"Do try the hors d'oeuvres. I learned to make them in the Far East," Estelle said to Meta. "You know I lived in Honolulu and Shanghai during my first marriage." She looked over at me. "I suppose you told her and Jerry." She continued to talk animatedly. "No one," she said, "even told me your last name."

Since the remark was obviously meant for Meta, I said, "Sorry, it's Carpenter."

"Oh, yes, of course," Estelle said, "I suppose, Miss Carpenter, you know all of the stars out here. Billy doesn't seem to care much about them, but I'd like to meet a few, go to the Trocadero to dance, and see what's the style with women in Hollywood. I still love to dance. Tell me, Miss Carpenter, do you go to Hollywood nightclubs often? Just what do you do? Billy said something about you working with Howard Hawks. Is that how you met my Billy?"

"Yes," Meta said coolly. "I work as a script girl with Mr. Hawks."

"Ben, I hope you take this pretty child out a lot."

I murmured something or other. Estelle rose quickly. "I'm having another martini," she said. "You'll have to join me. I fixed them myself."

Jerry praised the hors d'oeuvres. "Lots of curry," Estelle said.

A black woman entered, accompanied by a lovely, somewhat plump little girl.

"Here's my precious!" The child ran to her mother but called "Pappy" to Bill who was sitting across the room. Bill then took her around the room, introducing her and calling each adult by the first name, until he came to me and said "Uncle Ben."

Estelle told Jill, "Say goodnight to all the nice people." Jill made a charming curtsy, took her nurse's hand, and left us, followed by our exclamations of praise.

Estelle went to the martini pitcher. "Another round all around," she said. Only Jerry accepted. Then Estelle poured one for herself.

"Can't you persuade my husband to take me out to some of the nightclubs?" she said to Meta.

"I couldn't—" Meta began, but Estelle interrupted. "Oh, I'm sure you might be able to persuade him to take me. Or perhaps you can, Ben. He's always listened to you."

After dinner our host saw us to the door and we said good night to him. Jerry and Meta took me to my house. I don't believe we spoke a word to one another until we said good night.

My telephone rang early the next morning. It was Estelle, infuriated: "You didn't fool me for a second, you and Billy. I know that the person you brought to my house last night is Billy's girl out here and not your girl at all! I know about that movie actress you're so crazy about. I don't appreciate it one bit your flinging his mistress right in my face, and all these years you've been like a member of our family!" She hung up the receiver. If she hadn't, I don't know what I could have replied.

Then Bill phoned. "If Estelle called you up, I'm sorry. Ain't there something you can do to get her off my back?" He paused. "Get her a lover, anything, so she'll leave me alone."

I murmured platitudes, thinking this was surely the end of their marriage, but I was wrong.

Home—Greenville—for Christmas was my plan. Bill, in the midst of a writing assignment at a studio, accepted my invitation to move to my house while I was gone, where Paul could look after him and where he might use my car if he wished. Before I left Hollywood, I asked Anita Loos and her husband John Emerson—whom Bill had known in New Orleans—and Miriam Hopkins and a few others to invite him for lunch or dinner while I was away.

When I returned to my house after my vacation at home and the long train ride from Mississippi to California, I

Ben Wasson with Miriam Hopkins's son Michael, 1935

found Paul waiting for me in the courtyard. His woebegone expression made me immediately fearful that Bill had had another alcoholic session.

"Mr. Faulkner sick," Paul said.

"Drunk, Paul?"

"Drunk. Sick. Won't eat. I try to hide drink from him, but it don't do no good. Sorry," he said, as if I might blame him.

The house reeked with the stale odor of alcohol and cigarette smoke. Upstairs I found Bill stretched out on the couch in his undershorts. In the typewriter was a half-filled page. Thinking it might be a note to me, I read what Bill had typed; it was only a jumble of meaningless words.

"Couldn't get him to sleep in your room. More comfortable for him here, maybe."

"It's all right, Paul. Where are the bottles?" He wrung his small hands helplessly and his black eyes looked frightened.

"I'm sorry it happened, Paul, but do you know where the bottles are?"

"Can't find new ones. Old empty bottles everywhere." And so they were.

We searched for fresh unopened bottles, but I gave up the search for the time being and went to my room and unpacked my clothes.

"He take your car but not come home in it."

I notified the police who quickly located the car on Pico Boulevard. It was towed to a garage, looking like a well-plucked chicken, for the tires and some parts had been removed. And that was that.

Paul and I nursed Bill along, now and then getting him to eat something or drink milk. I noticed by now that when he went into the bathroom he came out smelling of wine. In the water tank of the commode I discovered he had stashed as many bottles of wine as the tank would hold. I didn't remove them since I knew he'd get more somewhere. Paul and I managed to reduce the amount he was consuming and to get him to drink from a glass instead of from the bottle.

The woman from whom I rented the house was a German who had not long been in this country. One afternoon she came to inquire about Bill, for Paul had told her he was ill. While she and I were talking, Bill came downstairs in an old dressing gown and sat on the sofa with a glass of wine in his hand. He joined in the conversation and was almost coy with her, several times lifting his glass to her and making a slight and foolish bow. I recall that she was an admirer of Hitler, who was then rising to power. Bill despised him, and they began to argue. I tried to change the subject to how well she maintained the court for her tenants.

Bill looked wretched. His complexion was pasty, his eyes red-rimmed, and his face half-covered in a grayish stubble of beard. He looked like a tramp. His robe had fallen open and his genitals were exposed. Our visitor couldn't help noticing, yet Bill didn't seem to care whether the robe was open or not. He continued to be almost cute with her. Paul came into the room and when he saw Bill's exposure he rushed to the kitchen, overcome with embarrassment. I could see that Bill was becoming tired. The glass fell from his hand, some of the wine spilling on the rug. He mumbled something about going upstairs to bed again and left us.

When he had gone, my landlady made clucking sounds like a hen. "*Sehr schlect*," she said, "too bad. Too much brains drive somebody to liquor maybe." Maybe, I agreed with her to myself, and too much liquor drives somebody else crazy.

"He's sick," I told her.

The next day, Paul and I took him to a hospital, as I should have done when I first returned from Greenville. When he was released, he was badly shaken and in a few days went home to Oxford.

Not long afterward I received a letter from him. He made an effort to explain why he drank so heavily, attributing much to despair and grief over his brother Dean's death in a recent airplane crash. He had persuaded Dean to join him in a commercial aviation business; otherwise, he said, Dean would be alive. There were other things which caused him to drink too much, he wrote. He declared he considered the letter he was writing to be a highly confidential one, written friend to friend, and would appreciate it if I destroyed it. I had Paul burn it for me in the incinerator.

"Buffie" (Elizabeth) Cobb, Irvin Cobb's only child, collaborated with me on a play, *Remember the Laughter*. The day it was completed I took it to Fredric March and his wife, Florence Eldridge. They acquired an option on it for a New York production. There was rewriting to be done, much of which I disapproved since it "hoked up" a play that had avoided a trite opening. I decided to return to Greenville until I was sent for to go to New York for rehearsals. But the play was never produced.

William Faulkner at home

At the same time, Bill was planning to go to Oxford in his new Ford. He invited me to accompany him on the cross-country trip. He was also taking another passenger, a black woman servant he had brought from Mississippi who wanted to return home. The day we were to leave Bill was late. Finally he arrived, and Paul helped me put my luggage in the car and off we started. Bill was fuming with anger.

On the way out of town he finally spoke. "Goddamn niggers, anyhow," he said. "You can't depend on a one of them. They expect everything and don't want to give anything back in return. I'm fed up with 'em, everyone of 'em. They're too triflin' to ever get anywhere."

"What's wrong?" I asked.

"Lucille decided she wanted to stay on out here. The very last minute she decided. To hell with her and all of 'em. We've got to get to Mississippi."

He drove extremely well, maintaining the correct speed and being always cautious.

"I reckon I flew off the handle back there, but like a fool I believed she wanted to go home. I reckon she's gotten herself tangled up with some big buck."

He didn't speak again until we reached the California-Arizona line. The terrain changed so drastically that nature had marked the two states in an incredible way. The California side was lush, green, and fertile. The Arizona side was, all at once, large boulders, brown, reddish colored.

"Look," I said, "as sudden as that, two completely different worlds. The abrupt change is extraordinary."

Bill stopped the car and viewed the scene for a while. "Maybe on the Arizona part they might put up a sign saying 'Science Fiction Country,' since it does look like scenery in a science fiction story. On the California side, I'd suggest a sign to read: 'Abandon hope, all ye who enter here,' or however Dante said it. Well, it's behind me for a while, anyhow."

He started the car motor again, but before putting it in gear he opened the glove compartment and took out a pint bottle of bourbon. Oh, Lordy, I said to myself. He offered the bottle to me, I shook my head, and he took a long drink, stoppered the bottle and put it on the seat between us. He became silent again. We drove and drove, and finally in the late afternoon we stopped at a tourist court. Those courts were rugged and uncouth when compared to the Holiday Inns, Ramadas, and Best Westerns available to travelers and tourists today. Bill drove the car to the small shack with the word "Office" on it. We went inside and approached an unkempt elderly room clerk at the table desk. Bill told him we needed a cabin for the night. Then he took the bottle from a coat pocket, drank, and passed it to the room clerk. He thanked Bill and poured a drink in a glass on the table. Then he showed us to a musty, wretchedly furnished room in a cabin. It had a bed in it, and that was all I cared about.

"Anything you want, come to the office," he told us, handing me the key.

"Where do we eat?" I asked.

"Got some sandwiches and a pot of coffee in my office," he said and left us.

The heat and stale air in the cabin were almost unbearable. Bill began to undress. I looked out the one window. Sand, sand, sand, stretching as far as I could see in the twilight. Bill stripped to his undershorts. He didn't say a word but took out the bottle, drank from it, and put it on the dresser. He got into bed, turned his back to the room, and grunted what may have been "Good night." I sat there until it was dark, then went to the office and ate a stale ham and cheese sandwich, which I washed down with the tepid cup of bitter coffee offered me by the clerk. I paid for the food, returned to the cabin, undressed in the dark, and climbed into bed beside my traveling companion who was sleeping soundly and loudly. I, too, was soon asleep with the knowledge that at least one day of travel was behind me but hardly looking forward to the remainder of the journey to Greenville.

The second day was similar to the first. It became hotter and hotter as we drove across the desert. The heat, the monotony of the scenery, the isolation, Bill's endless succession of bottles, and no conversation. I realized he was deeply unhappy for several reasons, most particularly Dean's death. I looked at his face once and noticed that his cheek was wet. We were both perspiring, but I knew the wetness on his cheek was tears. In the nights he sometimes called out Dean's name. There was no way for me to console him, and I had sense enough not to try. Even if we had run off the highway, it wouldn't have stopped his deep anguish.

We passed a group of Indians sitting beside the highway. They were dirty and had almost blind expressions in their eyes. Inanely, I said, "I wonder what Indians like that think about?"

"Whatever Indians think about," he replied. "No, I guess they do think about the bastard white man and how we robbed them of their heritage, treating them worse than cattle. This was theirs," he swept his arm in a wide gesture, "all of it. This whole country. We took it from them and shoved them off onto reservations. I reckon it's bad enough the way we treat the black folks. But they're like children and need looking after, expect to be looked after. Oh, hell, I don't know any answers for other people. I can't take care of my own problems."

It was the first time he had spoken at such length.

Once, I screwed up my courage and asked him how he felt about the critical reception of *Absalom, Absalom!* The reviews I had seen were harsh.

"I don't know what they said about it, but I'm told they didn't like it. But they don't know everything. Someday they'll grow up to that book. It's too much for them." He half grinned.

Clifton Fadiman's almost hysterically vitriolic review in *The New Yorker* must have been brought to Bill's attention, though he rarely sought out critical pieces about himself or his work. "I did think Fadiman's review was pretty funny. They seem to think I ought to be mad at him. He's got to eat, too. I do know, though, Bud, that *Absalom* is the last big one I'll write. It takes too much out of me." It was not the last big one, though.

The only planned stopover of the trip was in El Paso. All the other places where we spent a night had been somewhere we reached when night fell or where Bill wearied of driving. He wouldn't, at any time, let me take the wheel and relieve him of what I realize must have been a tiring and tedious grind. But in El Paso we were stopping over-night so that Bill could be with his brother Murry again. Murry had been with the Federal Bureau of Investigation for many years. There was a close bond among all the brothers—Bill, Murry, John, and Dean—and Dean's death had broken it. Murry was waiting in the hotel where he had made a reservation for us. What a relief it was to be in a decent modern hotel and not again in the first handy tourist court at the end of a long day on the road.

We went to our room. We had a drink, Murry raising his eyebrows at me when Bill took one. I knew what the ques-tioning eyebrows meant, and I nodded. Bill and Murry talked family, but mostly about Dean and his wife and about the baby girl whom Dean had not lived to see. I felt like an intruder to their intimate family talk.

After a while, Murry suggested that we go across the river to a Mexican restaurant. We walked over the bridge into Mexico, where he led us to a pleasant place that served good food and bottles of icy-cold Carta Blanca beer. The food and beer did Bill and me much good. I knew that for the first time since we had started cross-country I wasn't about to snap with tension.

"I reckon I'll have to go back to Hollywood again," Bill told his brother. "The more you make of that damn money, the more you have to make. Instead of being better off with that outrageous money they pay you, you become worse off."

We returned to the hotel, and I made an excuse to leave the brothers so that they could talk alone. I stayed away for an hour, walking about the town. When I returned, Murry had gone and Bill was already asleep. The next morning, in the car, Bill didn't reach for the pint bottle after we had gotten underway. At least I knew we were now headed for home. Fort Worth. Dallas. Shreveport. Across the bridge and the marvelous Mississippi River. Then the Delta and the plantations beginning to whiten with cotton. He had tapered off the booze now, and I felt better about him.

Then we were on my street in Greenville. He slowly drew up in front of our house. He cut off the motor. Darkness was beginning to fall. I looked at the house. There was no one at home. Out, I knew, for a late afternoon drive.

Bill asked me to telephone Estelle and tell her he was headed for Oxford. "And please," he added, "tell her I'm just fine. Give your family my love," he said, "and thanks for coming with me. I couldn't have made it without you. Come to Oxford when you want to and stay with us at Rowan Oak."

I got out of the car and removed my luggage. He switched on the motor and held up a hand. I said good-bye and he drove off down the street.

That was August, 1937. It would be several years before I would see Bill again.

Home Again

Life was hop, skip, and jump beginning with 1941 when I joined the U. S. Navy and served for three years. Upon my discharge, I returned to Greenville for several months, then went to New York, then back to Greenville, where I remained almost continuously.

The visits Bill and I had from 1944 until 1956 were in Greenville and Oxford mostly. When I first saw him again following my settling in Greenville, I realized that he had changed. His hair was flecked with white but was still quite thick. His moustache, which he wore at different lengths from time to time, was also gray. His body had thickened considerably. He still held himself "proudlike," and his eyes seemed to me to be more penetrating than I had remembered, and his lips were thinner. He talked in a quite worldly manner, altogether more urbanely. He still laughed often and had not lost his characteristic chuckle, and his risibility was generally brought about by human foibles, bucolic humor, and chicanery.

Shelby Foote, born and reared in Greenville, had decided when he completed his military service that he would live there. His ambition was to become a professional author, and his favorite living writer was William Faulkner. He admired everything Bill had written and recognized that Faulkner was a truly dedicated writer. I told Bill of Shelby's desire to meet him, and he invited us to come to Rowan Oak for supper and to spend the night at the Sigma Alpha Epsilon house on the Ole Miss campus.

Estelle, the ebullient and perfect hostess, welcomed us. "Billy and Jill are puttering out there in the barn, whatever that means. Lord knows, they spend enough time out there." She led us to the parlor, which adjoined the dining room.

Across from the entrance hall was Bill's sitting room, with a workroom and study behind it. His sitting room was casual and simply furnished, and his workroom was bare except for those few things necessary to his writing—table, typewriter, and other appurtenances. It was free of decoration, as was his sitting room, except for the portrait of Bill painted by his mother which hung over the mantel. It was an attractive painting of a youth, clear-eyed and innocent-faced, and there was great sweetness in the portrait.

The parlor was a more formal room, and Estelle customarily used it when visitors came to call. In it were a number of oriental hangings and other objects that many years before she had brought back to Oxford from China when she and Cornell Franklin ended their marriage.

Estelle introduced Bill and Shelby to each other, and it was immediately obvious that the two men, the older author and the young man just beginning to become one, liked each other. Estelle went to bring us drinks, saying to Bill, "I'll bring you your beer, Pappy."

"Sit down," Bill said, getting out his tobacco pouch and pipe and gesturing toward chairs. "How's the cotton in the Delta?"

"Looks good," Shelby said. "It might be a fine year."

"Delta planters!" Bill said. "No wonder it grows like a wand's been waved over it, with all that good silt the Mississippi River's spread so many years."

"How's your farm?" Shelby said.

"Oh, I ain't in the class with you Delta planters. I just have a small dirt farm. Got to scratch for what I get out of it—beans, corn." He suggested that we go on the side porch, overlooking a rose garden, where it was cooler. "That's Estelle's doing. She's good with all kinds of flowers. Has a sho-nuff green thumb." He rambled on, talking about how pioneer women carried flower cuttings with them on their hard journey to new and unbroken land. "The men brought in the meat, and the women the flowers."

Estelle brought the drinks, and we talked of family and mutual friends. A table on the porch had been laid for supper, which Estelle served after we finished our drinks. Shelby complimented Estelle on her centerpiece of roses and lighted candles.

"Just the old-fashioned roses. I don't go in much for the newfangled varieties," she said with a bright smile, and added, "Shelby, I hope you have a girl."

"No, ma'am, not a special one, Mrs. Faulkner."

"And you, Ben? Whatever became of your movie star romance? I read about it in the movie magazines, and Louella Parsons wrote about it, too, didn't she?"

"Those days seem long ago, now," I said.

"Hollywood," Bill half-mumbled.

"Pappy never likes it when he has to go out there, but he says he has to make that money." She moved to another subject. "Shelby, I tried my hand at a novel a long time ago, but Ben and Billy both said it wasn't good enough, so I stopped trying." Her mouth dropped petulantly. "Pappy, why don't you get a bottle of wine for our supper?"

When Bill poured the wine, he lifted his glass and made a slight bow. "*A votre santé*," he said. "*Bon appétit*." Then he bowed his head and said a blessing for the meal, and supper proceeded pleasantly with inconsequential talk.

Shelby Foote not long ago reminded me of two bits of conversation from that late afternoon. At some point, and before Shelby and I departed for the SAE house, Estelle asked Bill to tell us what their cook said about the yard man.

Bill laughed. "She said, 'He puts me to mind of a long, dusty black snake, just run out from under a stump.'"

Also, Shelby asked Bill about Sherwood Anderson and the times in New Orleans, and Bill replied, "In those days down there in the French Quarter, Sherwood Anderson reminded me of a coach horse, because of the flashy clothes he wore."

When Shelby published *Tournament*, his first novel, and sent Bill a complimentary copy, Bill remarked to me, "Good stuff in it. If Shelby ever gets over my influence on him as a writer, he'll be just fine."

Today, Shelby is a distinguished novelist and historian, particularly noted for his three-volume *The Civil War: A Narrative*.

Shelby Foote's visit with me to Rowan Oak was only one of several I made there. Sometimes I went alone, and on other occasions I took someone who was eager to meet Bill.

Hodding Carter (nicknamed "Big" by his family) and Bill wished to meet; so Hodding and I set out for Oxford. The two men talked about general affairs but soon enough came specifically to the burning question at the moment: "Shall the South integrate or remain segregated?"

Before they had gotten into the matter, Bill suggested that we have toddies. He left us and brought back a tray with sugar water, bourbon, and ice. He was followed by a black houseman, who waited while Bill prepared the drinks. "Toddies have to be carefully made," Bill said, "and the sugar water has to be exactly right. I always keep a supply on hand."

He fixed the drinks, handing one to Hodding, one to me,

and one to the servant, then took one for himself. The
servant stood in the doorway, slowly drinking his toddy as
the three of us enjoyed ours.

"I'm using an elderly black man as a detective in a book
I'm now writing," Bill said. We asked him to tell us about
it.

"It's a combination mystery and detective novel with, I
hope, excitement in the plot. There's been a murder, and
an elderly white gentlewoman and young boys approaching
manhood solve the mystery of how the body of the mur-
dered man is changed in his burial place. I've had a hell of a
good time writing it, but I haven't thought of a title for it.
Maybe one of you might have an idea and come up with the
right title that'll fit the plot."

We told him we'd try to think of something.

The houseman inquired of Bill if there was something for
him to do, and he was thanked and dismissed. After he left
the room, Bill said, "I always invite him to have a toddy
with me whenever I have one. They're a part of our
families, ain't they?"

Several years later, on November 10, 1955, at a Southern Historical Association meeting in Memphis, where Bill
was one of three speakers, his talk was titled "American
Segregation and the World Crisis." Here is the opening
paragraph:

> For the moment and for the sake of the argument, let's say
> that, as a white Southerner and maybe even any white Ameri-
> can, I too curse the day when the first Negro was brought
> against his will to this country and sold into slavery. Because
> that doesn't matter now. To live anywhere in the world of A.
> D. 1955 and be against equality because of race or color, is like
> living in Alaska and being against snow.

In this speech he was moving from his first refusal to
accept anything but a token integration. The speech led to
great criticism by many of his closest friends and caused a

Oxford premiere of *Intruder in the Dust*, October 1949

breach in his family, some of whom considered he had "gone too far."

At any rate, Bill wanted a title for the book, and I wrote him from Greenville a few days later offering one or two suggestions that he didn't accept, but he thanked me and asked that I keep trying to think of one he'd like. He soon wrote that he had come up with *Intruder in the Dust*.

A movie version of the novel was filmed in Oxford and had its premiere showing there with much attendant hullabaloo. It was generously reviewed in Hodding Carter's Greenville newspaper, the *Delta Democrat-Times*, by Elizabeth Spencer, another fine Mississippi author.

Among those who visited Betty and Hodding Carter's lovely home, Feliciana, were not only citizens of the United States but also Europeans who sought Hodding's opinions, especially his thoughts about the race question.

One, a young Englishman with the BBC, wanted to meet Bill and Estelle, so I telephoned Rowan Oak and was told to bring him over.

Again we sat on the side porch. Estelle, the eternal belle, told me Jill was at her Grandmother Oldham's, and her son Malcolm, she said, was likely "out in some old ditch, looking for snakes." He was eager to become a herpetologist. "He wouldn't want to be anything normal like a lawyer, or anything useful like a plumber or a bootlegger," she said, laughing.

The drinks had been passed around and when conversation was lagging, I suggested that we play CALVERT. The object of the game was that for each letter in that word one must give the name of a United States president whose name began with that letter. It seemed easy and we quickly named a president for all letters except *E*. We tried and tried but couldn't recall one. Bill, who was becoming vexed, went into the house and brought out the *E* volume of an encyclopedia, but we continued our search without luck.

"Damn it," he said. "They shouldn't have made up a game with such an error." He turned to the visitor and asked him what his profession was, and the man answered, "I am a journalist." Bill's mouth tightened, and he got up and left us. Estelle and I knew that he suspected the journalist wished to invade his treasured privacy. Estelle valiantly chattered away. As she questioned the visitor about England, he suddenly interrupted her. "I know who it is!" "The *E* is for *Eisenhower!*" he exclaimed.

"Of course, it's *Eisenhower*," I said. "He hasn't been president long enough for us to think of him or to be in an encyclopedia."

Bill joined us, somewhat recovered from his pique, and Estelle jubilantly told him whom the *E* stood for. She then served an excellent curried chicken, and Bill, as was his custom, made the salad dressing, pointing out that only the highest quality of olive oil should be used in careful proportion to the lemon juice.

It now is somewhat difficult for me to believe that throughout the years that I went to Oxford I saw Bill and Phil Stone—his oldest friend, adviser, and benefactor—together only one or two times. But Phil once talked with me about Bill. I was in Oxford, and Estelle had asked me to Rowan Oak for lunch. Bill and Jill, now a charming young girl whose birthday it happened to be, were at the luncheon table. After lunch, I strolled into town, where I encountered Phil Stone on the square. He invited me to have a drink with him, and we went to his law office, which was situated off the square in a mellowing red brick one-story building. Phil almost immediately began talking about Bill's newest manuscript, which was to become *A Fable*.

"I'm afraid it's a lot of gibberish, from what I know about it," Phil said. "Bill must have slipped a mental groove to be writing such stuff. He won't listen to me when I try to tell him he's gotten way off the track."

"What's it about?" I asked.

"It's about Jesus appearing during a battle in World War II and about how the soldiers lay down their arms, and a lot of other puzzling events. I can't do a thing with him. When I talk to him about it, he clasps his lips together—you know how he does when he gets set about something—and won't talk at all."

I changed the subject, finished my drink, thanked him for his hospitality, and said good-bye.

On the way back to Rowan Oak, I stopped at a flower shop and purchased a small corsage of sweetheart roses for Jill. She thanked me, and her father told me that it was the first corsage she had ever received. "Did you see Stone?" Bill asked. I told him I had. "He's telling anyone who'll listen to him that I'm writing a lot of drivel. I'm sorry, but I don't see Stone as much as I used to. He's always telling me how I ought to write, whatever I'm writing."

Some years later Phil Stone's mind broke down, and he spent his last days at Whitfield, the state hospital near Jackson.

Hodding Carter, Kenneth Haxton, Jr. (a young, local merchant and musician-composer) and I were partners in founding the Levee Press to publish limited editions of books by Mississippians. We composed the entire staff. None of us knew very much about publishing books. Our plan was to print them on the presses of Carter's newspaper, the *Delta Democrat-Times*, and we had purchased special types of fonts for the purpose. A company in Texas was commissioned to bind the books, each of which was to be numbered and signed by its author.

In 1948, the Levee Press published its first book. I had brazenly asked Eudora Welty if she would permit the new publishing firm to issue one of her manuscripts as a book and had told her the plans for the new press. The great and gracious lady replied that she approved of such a venture, that Mississippi needed a limited editions press, and that, as it happened, she did have a manuscript. It was a novella, *Music from Spain*. I asked her please to send it and soon she did. The three partners who made up the firm were more than delighted to have the opportunity of publishing this distinguished and winsome story, with its delicate ironical overtones. It made a great start for the Levee Press.

Music from Spain, when completed, was signed by Miss Welty and was priced at four dollars a copy, an exorbitant charge for so small a book at that time. It is now a collector's item. Soon after the publication of *Music from Spain*, I wrote Bill, asking if he would consider letting us have a

Hodding Carter, Kenneth Haxton, and Ben Wasson, owners of
the Levee Press

Eudora Welty

manuscript. He answered quickly, declaring that he heartily approved the idea behind the formation of the Press. He said that he would go through his unpublished manuscripts and see if he had something that might be suitable. He invited Hodding and me to come over and talk about it.

So we went to Rowan Oak again. He was alone when we arrived, and this time he gave us our choices of highballs: Scotch or bourbon. Again the talk revolved around the integration question, and that afternoon the three of us agreed that the last holdouts against integration would be three or four Southern states, including Mississippi. Hodding and Bill also agreed that Mississippi and the New England states were the states that were least subject to change of any kind. Hodding maintained that these were homogeneous to a great degree. Bill had written a few letters to the Memphis *Commercial Appeal* and to the Oxford *Eagle*, the first of these letters making expressions against integration. But the letters soon expressed a more amenable attitude, until finally he did a complete about-face on the subject.

When I brought up the subject of the Levee Press, Bill said that as it happened he did have a completed unpublished manuscript, a novella that would ultimately become an integral part of the long novel on which he was working. He proposed that we take the section back home with us and that, if we decided to use it, he thought that "A Long Dangling Clause from a Work in Progress" might be a fitting and provocative title for it.

He handed us a manila envelope. "Maybe you can use it and maybe not," he said, and Hodding and I smiled at each other. All the way back to Greenville, we were in a state of great elation. The acquisition of the Faulkner manuscript was truly a literary coup for the Levee Press.

Kenneth Haxton, too, was delighted with our acquisition, and plans went forward, though not without delays, to get it printed and bound. We titled it *Notes on a Horsethief* and selected a grass-green binding with the imprint of a horse's head in silver. The type was set in green ink. Elizabeth Calvert did the drawings for the end papers, as well as two other illustrations. Galley proofs had to be read, a task Bill abhorred but which he consented to do. Josephine Haxton, Kenneth's wife—Ellen Douglas, now a critically acclaimed writer—and Betty Carter and Kenneth himself also checked proofs. It was a fiendish job of proofing, what with Bill's eccentric punctuation and innovations, and despite meticulous checking, not all errors were eliminated. The pages were forwarded to the bindery, and after a time the books arrived at the *Delta Democrat-Times*. I wrote Bill telling him of their arrival.

Without advance notice, he came a few days later to Greenville, driving directly to the newspaper office. He was delighted with the book and its all-around appearance. I got help from several in the office and we scurried about, placing the boxes of *Notes on a Horsethief* in Hodding's office for autographing, where Bill, in his careful organizational way arranged what he called an assembly line, with himself in the role of boss man. A young woman employee of the *Democrat* joined him and me in the line. I removed the books from boxes; Bill signed and numbered each copy, then passed it on to the young woman, who blotted the signatures and numbers and returned the copies to boxes. It all went smoothly, particularly since Hodding had provided a generous supply of cold beer.

As we were about to wind up the job, Kenneth, knowing how much Bill liked fish, led Bill and me to a seafood restaurant. "Great God amighty, they ain't any better eatin' than this," Bill said, as he peeled and ate quantities of cold boiled shrimp.

Hodding and Betty were entertaining visitors that entire

day and couldn't be with us. He did, though, write about Bill's two-day visit. This highly amusing account appeared first in his *Where Main Street Meets the River*. It is a longer account than I have given here and is much more expertly told.

Bill and I went that night to Doe's Eat Place for steaks. He enjoyed Doe's and its unpretentiousness and superb food. He continued to praise everything about what the Levee Press had accomplished in printing *Notes*. He especially admired the cover, the horse's head, and the green ink. After dinner, we went to see a Greenville lawyer Bill had known at Ole Miss before I went there. He was noted for his "dry" wit, but he was, at the time we went to his house, a Sunday School teacher and talked religion to Bill. "I believe," Bill said as we drove away from the lawyer's house, "I liked his dry wit better when he was a drinker than his wet wit now that he's a dry."

Next morning we boarded Hodding's cabin cruiser, *Mister Charley*, for a leisurely ride on Lake Ferguson and from there went on into the Mississippi River. John Gibson, business manager of the *Delta Democrat-Times*, was at the wheel, but he turned it over to the guest when we got into the river channel. Bill steered the boat expertly and admired it. In the role of pilot he was as happy as a small boy as he scanned the surging water and the Arkansas and Mississippi sides with an air of authority.

Hodding wondered aloud if the river would ever be tamed.

"Not this Old Man," Bill said, just as I had heard him say it before. "Won't ever be tamed."

Hodding was serving drinks, and I knew, or feared, that Bill might well be headed for a spree, and as soon as the boat docked, I'm afraid I didn't urge him to linger in Greenville.

Copies of *Notes on a Horsethief* were mailed the next

day. The few critics who reviewed it were warm though puzzled in their praise, and the edition of 750 copies was quickly sold out at six dollars per copy.

Before Bill started for Oxford after the boat ride, he said he wanted to stop by the house and say good-bye to my mother. He had several copies of *Notes*, and when we were at the house, after visiting awhile with Mother, he gave me two copies, one for Mother, the other for Ruth.

The one to Ruth, in recollection of their talks when she was four, reads: "Dear Ruth—in its fashion it is a pair of silver slippers. William Faulkner, Greenville, Jan. 20, 1951." The one to my mother reads: "For Mrs. Wasson, with love. A lady who has remained completely unspoiled by my success. Bill Faulkner, Greenville, 20 Jan. 1951."

On an unplanned trip to Oxford, when I telephoned Rowan Oak, Bill told me to come out and visit. Estelle was not at home, but the cook told me to go to the barn where "Mr. Bill" was doing some carpentry. The barn was only a short distance from the house, and as I approached, I was greeted by shrill yelps from a feisty dog. Bill had a fancy for that small, shrilly yapping type of dog. "Hush up, dog," Bill called out, putting down his hammer. "Come on, Ben, he just makes a lot of noise. Sit on those boards," he said, indicating a nearby stack of lumber. "I'll be through with this job in a few minutes." And he began hammering a nail into a board at the side of the barn. The nail bent. "Damn it to hell, nobody takes pride in anything they make nowadays. Even nails ain't any good. The day for artisans is over. Shoddy is the word for what's made now." He had the greatest respect for simple things well made. He did most of the repair work necessary at both Rowan Oak and his farm.

He paused and said, "You know, Bud, maybe I'd have

done a better job as a carpenter than as a writer." He hammered for a few moments and added, "I expect Jesus was a first-rate carpenter, not a jackleg artisan."

By now Estelle had returned. She called to us to come to the house, and the little dog commenced yapping at me again and making tiny lunges at me. "Hush up, dog, and get out of the way. Where are your manners?"

After we had chatted with Estelle, Bill and I rode to town, and he called my attention to the great number of TV aerials on roofs. "I'm willing to bet," he said, "that most of those aren't attached to television sets. These folks don't own any. But they like to have their neighbors think they do. Another American status symbol. Keeping up with the Joneses. If it makes 'em happy, so be it. I don't want a television set in my house and hear it squawking all day and night."

Later, he relented and purchased a modest, black and white set for Rowan Oak. For a time, however, he went every Sunday to Dr. James Silver's house and looked at a particular program he fancied. "Awful stuff," Jim Silver told me. "He sits there in front of the TV, puffs away at his pipe, and watches and listens intently. He never says a word about the program, and when it's over he thanks me and leaves."

On that day when we were riding around, he told me a story—a good example of the kind of humor he relished. "It seems," he said, "that two creatures from outer space were flying over an American city, and one of them looked down at the roofs below with the aerials on them and said, 'Look at all those good-looking females down there.'" He began laughing and for a while seemed unable to contain his amusement.

By tradition, the weather for Delta Council Day, which is held annually in Cleveland, Mississippi, has always been glorious. May 15, 1952, was no exception. The Delta Council is composed of cotton planters who are dedicated to furthering the interests of the cotton industry. The membership also includes bankers, lawyers, leading merchants, physicians, and most of the prominent white Delta citizens. Each year hundreds of members and their guests come to the campus of Delta State University to renew friendships, listen to prominent speakers, and eat barbecue. Among the speakers have been United States secretaries of state, treasury, agriculture, senators and congressmen, presidents of the United States Chamber of Commerce, prominent generals, authors—always people holding positions of importance and influence.

The speakers in 1952 were Governor James F. Byrnes of South Carolina and William Faulkner, recent Nobel Prize recipient and native son whom the state of Mississippi could hold in high esteem. There were, of course, several people at the gathering that day who remembered him as Count No 'Count. I was invited to "stick around" and make him feel at home.

It was pleasant to be with him again. He was dressed quite well, and I complimented him on the cream silk shirt he wore. He told me he had had it made out of parachute silk. I noticed that the collar was quite frayed, but, even so, he appeared most distinguished, with his special air that important and basically simple and natural people have. He had his own sartorial elegance. He, like others present, wore a rather large plastic nameplate, this beneath the rosette of the French Legion of Honor. He seemed quietly elated, and as we sat at a bare table eating barbecue and potato salad from paper plates, many friends and others came to speak to him or to introduce themselves. He greeted everyone in a low, soft voice, and in a dignified, polite way he thanked them for their compliments on his success as an author and gave autographs when requested and permitted snapshots to be taken.

He spoke to me of the people wandering about the spacious grounds at the college. It was a custom of the Council to give awards to the best-dressed man and best-dressed woman present who were wearing cotton clothing. "They're not," he said, "a bit like the farmers in my part of Mississippi. These Delta folks all *look* rich. There's something about them suggesting Midas must have touched them. Rich like the Delta soil. Rich. Productive. And maybe self-satisfied. The hill folks think all you people are godless and headed for fire and brimstone. I expect most Deltans are touched with hubris."

Shortly before the speechmaking began, we were led to the area behind the stage in the auditorium where he was to speak. As we sat there waiting to be summoned, David Brown of the *Delta Democrat-Times* and Bern Keating, a well-known free-lance photographer from Greenville, took pictures and asked him several questions. One of them asked what the word Yoknapatawpha meant in English.

"Not a thing," Bill answered. "I just made it up. Sounded right to me when I first thought of it, so I used it." (At other times he had been known to give meanings to the word he used as the name of his famous fictional county.) "I like to make up names, and I'm pretty good at it, don't you think?"

Then we were called to the stage. Bill was given a spontaneous standing ovation. Unfortunately, the public address system went awry, the wiring to the microphone being faulty, and only those within the immediate range of Bill's voice could hear his speech. The microphone issued hellish squeaking sounds. I, however, could hear most of what he said, and I cringed at a factual error he made. Near the conclusion of his address, he said: "I decline to believe that the only true heirs of Boone and Franklin and George

Ben Wasson and William Faulkner, Delta Council meeting, 1952

and Booker T. Washington and Lincoln and Jefferson and
Adams and John Henry and John Bunyan [he meant Paul
Bunyan] and Johnny Appleseed and Lee and Crockett and
Hale and Helen Keller, are the ones denying and protest-
ing in the newspaper headlines over mink coats and oil
tankers and federal indictments for corruption in public
office." It was a small mistake, and he corrected it when he
edited the manuscript for a pamphlet he permitted the
Council to print and send to its members. He said he was
satisfied with the speech.

Outside, he was surrounded by people congratulating
him on his address, though I doubt that many of them
heard it.

William T. (Billy) Wynn, a Greenville attorney who had
written Bill urging him to accept the council's invitation to
speak, came to us, shook Bill's hand, and said: "Since you
wouldn't accept a financial honorarium for your fine speech
today, we did what you requested and bought you a case of
'good drinking whiskey—bourbon.' It's been placed in the
trunk of your car, guarded until you get there."

Bill laughed, thanked him, and bowed, and we left the
campus and went to a local restaurant where we joined
several friends.

Soon afterward, on a warm day in summer, Bill returned to
Greenville, as usual unannounced. I was at home with my
sister, Mary Wilkinson, her husband, Charles, and my
mother. Bill carried a shabby, much worn briefcase. He set
it down and we shook hands.

"Here's the manuscript of my new novel, *A Fable*. I want
you to be the first to read it. I know it's my finest." He said
he wanted to see Mother, and I took him to her room. She
was now a semi-invalid, and he sat by her bed and they
teased each other. She asked about Jill's romances, but he

seemed evasive, merely saying "yes ma'am" and "no ma'am" to her questions. After they finished talking, he and I went into the living room.

Estelle and Jill, he told me, were in Mexico City where Jill was attending the University of Mexico for a short while. He had disagreed with her about a young man she fancied. He didn't go into details, and there had been no real breach between them, but I assumed they had decided that some time apart would be a good idea.

He nodded toward the briefcase. "I've put everything I have into that one. It sure took it out of me, but I found out the sap's still in me even if it surges slower and more painfully now. I do want your opinion."

"Is this the one in which you're using the story about the horse we used for the Levee Press?" *Notes on a Horsethief*, of course.

"The same, and I didn't have to make too many changes. Say," he added abruptly, "haven't you got something in the house to drink—and not a Coca-Cola?"

I asked if a beer would be all right. He said it would, and I got him one out of the refrigerator.

"That was a hot ride over here," he said. "My yard boy drove me and is waiting in the car. You know a place where he can spend the night?"

I told him there was a hotel on Nelson Street for blacks— this was before integration—and that I would lead the way and his driver could follow us.

"Let's take my boy to that hotel." He got up, set the beer glass down, and we went to the car. He introduced me to his young chauffeur and instructed him to follow us. With Bill beside me, I drove to Nelson Street, a small version of Memphis's Beale Street, and stopped at a two-story brick building which had a sign proclaiming that it was El

Morooco. Bill found this misspelling amusing. He instructed his driver, who looked to be about twenty years old, to behave himself and to telephone him at my house the next morning. "Now don't you get into any scrapes," he admonished as we left, and I thought the black youth looked lost and forlorn.

"A good enough boy, I reckon," Bill said, "and I hope to God he don't get into trouble tonight. Say, can't we go somewhere and buy some bourbon?"

I realized that it was useless for me to protest, so I took him to a place that sold liquor illegally, Mississippi then being a dry state. On the way he told me that he had asked Estelle, while she was in Mexico, to get in touch with Bill Spratling, his old friend from New Orleans days. Spratling had become a successful businessman, having established a silver and tin business in Taxco. Then he changed the subject. "Sorry you've gone teetotal on me, Bud." I saw that Bill was quite nervous.

He was silent as we drove down the highway toward the liquor store, passing along between acres and acres of cotton and plantation tenant cabins. On the porch of one of them, there was a washing machine. Without any preamble, he said, "Now they don't even have a tub of washing to do every day to keep them out of trouble. They just throw their dirty laundry in an electric machine and go on about their business—and everybody else's business, too." This remark reminded me of the one he made years before when he had been so angry about his mother's meddling in his royalty arrangements.

We bought the liquor and then drove back to the house where I fixed him a highball. I then told him I was invited to a dinner party that night and wondered if he cared to go, for I was certain that the hostess would be glad to have him. He surprised me by agreeing to go. I telephoned the hostess, Mrs. Allew Haycraft, a dear and lovely friend, and she was delighted that Bill would be a guest.

Charlie and my sister had come home, and Bill and I joined them in the living room. Charlie, too, had a drink, and he and Bill held a rambling conversation about art, Bill declaring that da Vinci was the greatest artist who ever lived, Charlie claiming Michelangelo was the greatest.

At the Greenville Country Club we were greeted by our hostess, who led us to a private room. She introduced Bill to the twelve guests already assembled, and I was pleased to notice that most of the men had been pilots in World War II, for Bill loved to talk about flying. Drinks were being passed, along with appetizers, and conversation was genial and animated. Bill seemed at home, with the former pilots questioning him about his barnstorming days, the types of planes used, and how many pilots were engaged in the business with him. These air force men had been stationed at the Greenville Air Force Base and had married Greenville women. Several of them were Easterners, and one an Englishman. Feeling comfortable with the guests, Bill opened up, and it was obvious that everyone there was finding him gracious.

At the table, he recounted a number of delightful stories of his own flying experience, but he said nothing of his service with the RAF in World War I. I never heard him mention that subject in those later years. During dinner several young people had peered into the room. They had heard that William Faulkner, the Nobel Prize winner, was present, and they wanted to see him. But none of them asked for an autograph.

At the conclusion of the meal, Mrs. Haycraft invited everyone to come to her home, a beautiful house, where we could have liqueurs. I feared for us to go to Mrs. Haycraft's, since I felt certain, by then, that Bill was on the way to another long siege of drinking. Bern Keating was there with his charming wife, Franke, and at my suggestion they invited everyone to their house instead. At the Keatings' informal attractive house, Bern and Franke passed drinks. No one by then was, as the saying goes, feeling any pain, and Bill was the most convivial one in the group. Several of the guests had gone home since it had been after midnight when we left the Country Club. I was tired, and ready to go home myself, but Bill wanted to stay awhile with the Keatings, saying that someone could take him to a motel. Bern and Franke invited him to spend the night, and he accepted immediately. Greatly worried, I told him I'd see him later in the morning. "Maybe we'll go down to Biloxi," Bill said.

About seven o'clock that morning I answered the telephone. "Mr. Faulkner," Franke Keating said in almost a whisper, "fell down in the kitchen sometime in the night and cut his head. It bled a great deal, but we stopped the bleeding, and he's asleep now." I told her I would come immediately.

"The house looks awful," Franke apologized when she met me at the door, "but who's had time to bother about clearing up this cyclone?"

"He bled a lot," Bern said.

"My God," Franke said, "maybe we should have called a doctor. We hated to call you and wake up your mother. He got up around three o'clock, wasn't it, Bern?"

Bern corroborated the time, and then the two, interrupting each other, told me they had been awakened by a crash from the kitchen, where they found Bill lying on the floor near the sink.

"We put on a bandage," Bern said.

"We managed to stop the bleeding by putting ice on the

Bern and Franke Keating

cut," Franke said. "Look at his tie." A bloodied tie was hanging on a kitchen rack. "Don't look at this kitchen."

"Where is he now?" I asked.

"Sound asleep in the guest room," Bern said.

"I made him take two aspirins," Franke added.

I looked in the guest room. The injured house-guest, his forehead bandaged, was snoring.

In the living room, where Franke brought coffee to Bern and me, we held a consultation, the upshot of which was my decision to get Bill to a Greenville hospital or to take him back to Oxford. The Keatings offered to take him in their car, and I was to accompany them. When Bill awakened, Bern and I got him dressed and told him we were going to Oxford.

"Let's go to the Coast," Bill kept saying.

We first had to pick up his driver, and I had to stop by my house, tell my family I was going to Oxford, and leave my car with them. With Bill half asleep, we got him in the back seat, and after the stop at my house, we went to the El Morooco. Bill's driver was waiting at the entrance. He was in dire shape, his clothes torn, and, judging from an eye, he had been in a fight. He wore a hangdog expression. I told him what he was to do, and he said he would stay close behind us to Oxford.

Bill was sleeping soundly, and Franke, Bern, and I on the front seat said very little to one another, hoping Bill wouldn't awaken. However, we had been underway only a short while, when he sat up and asked where we were going. I told him we were going to Oxford, and he said crossly, "I want to go to Biloxi." I told him we'd first stop at Rowan Oak, and he lay back on the seat. He awoke again and asked for whiskey. Bern gave me the bottle which we had brought with us, and I handed it to Bill. Then he lapsed into sleep.

Intermittently he woke up and leaned toward Franke: "You sure are pretty," and beamed at her foolishly. Several times he demanded that Bern and I help him from the car. "I gotta take a piss," he'd mumble. Bern or I would lead him from the car and to a sheltered place along the highway. He would get back into the car, leer at Franke and say, "You sure are pretty," and go to sleep, then wake up and demand that we go to the Mississippi Gulf Coast.

Followed by the Faulkner chauffeur, we pulled in at Rowan Oak. It was late afternoon and a red glow colored the white-pillared house and the cedar-lined drive. Bill awakened as soon as we arrived, got out of the car, and seemed almost sober. Taking the whiskey, he led us inside and, now the perfect host, told us to make ourselves at home. He said he regretted that Estelle was not there to welcome us.

For a time we sat in the parlor, and with every minute

Bill seemed to become more sober. Finally, he suggested
that we drive to town where Franke who had volunteered
to prepare supper for us could shop for what she needed.

At the square, Franke and Bern exclaimed at the beauty
of the courthouse, which they knew well as the Jefferson
courthouse in Faulkner's stories and novels. Bill said indignantly that "folks are trying to tear away the galleries at the
storefronts, and the Victorian ornamentations. Ruin it all,
damn it." I knew that he had written letters of protest
about the destruction of the older buildings.

Bill took us to the drugstore owned by Mac Reed, his
longtime friend and confidant, and introduced Franke and
Bern to him. Mac and I already knew each other, and,
when he had an opportunity, he inquired of me, "Drinking?" I nodded. "I thought so," he said.

After Bern and Mac had talked, Bill took us to a nearby
grocery store, and Franke bought what she needed. Seeming quite sober now, Bill got into Bern's car with us, and
we returned to Rowan Oak.

We were taken this time to Bill's sitting room, rather
than the parlor, and from the sitting room he took us to his
study. The white plaster walls were almost covered by
seven outlines in black ink—at least it looked like ink.

"What in the world are those?" Bern exclaimed.

"They're outlines of each of the seven days of my new
novel. It was easier for me to keep up with the time of
action by having them on the wall before me."

"Jesus Christ!" Bern exclaimed. In an aside to me, he
said, "Ask Faulkner if I may take a picture of them." Bill
said of course for Bern to go ahead and take the pictures.
They turned out well and later Bern sold a part of them to
Life magazine.

Bill showed Franke the kitchen and told her to feel free
to use anything she needed. In the study Bern commented

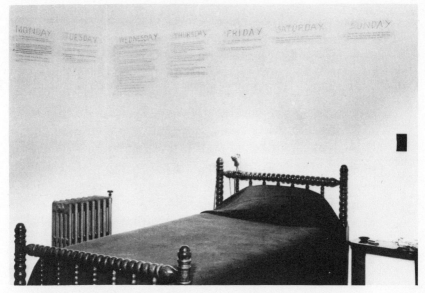

Faulkner's outline for *A Fable*

on the painting above the fireplace, the one Miss Maud had done of Bill as a young man. "My mother still paints and is quite good, I think," Bill said with pride.

While he told Bern how he had come to purchase Rowan Oak, I looked at the books in the shelves, seeing many of the classics and several volumes of poetry, both old and modern. Franke announced supper and led the way to the dining room. Before we sat down, Bill excused himself and returned with a bottle. "I think Franke's meal deserves a bottle of wine with it," he said.

"It's just a salad, a sandwich, and sherbet for dessert. And a store-bought cake I'm afraid," Franke said. She had lit the candles on the table, and Bill poured the wine. Then, he mixed the salad dressing, with his usual ceremony. The three of us were very hungry, and Bill drank several glasses of wine. He became quite jovial and flirted with Franke.

Soon after supper, he led us upstairs, then went into his room and closed the door. We selected rooms in which to sleep. I was in a room that must have been used sometimes by Bill, for there was a pipe in the ashtray and many paperback books were on the bedside table, mostly mystery and detective novels.

Bern and I made certain that Bill was undressed and sleeping before we went to bed. It wasn't by any stretch of the imagination a restful night. We were not familiar with the bedrooms. The light bulbs were of low wattage, and much of the upper part of the house was in the shadows. Mosquitoes buzzed around us. It was hot with no breeze stirring. I heard Bill going up and down the stairs during the night, which, altogether was phantasmagoric. Quite late, I finally slept. The next morning I was awakened by the pleasant aroma of coffee brewing.

Franke was already in the kitchen and preparing breakfast for us. I telephoned Bill's stepson Malcolm Franklin and told him why I was in Oxford. Bill was still asleep. While we were eating breakfast, Malcolm came to Rowan Oak, and in low voices we told him of the past two nights.

Malcolm assured us he would look after his stepfather, as he'd done at other times. "Pappy just got lonesome with Mama and Jill away," he said, "and he'd finished writing that new book of his."

I told Malcolm—kind, gentle Malcolm—that the manuscript was in safekeeping at our house in Greenville. He hadn't known that Bill had gone to Greenville to see me. Bill didn't wake up before we left for home.

Before Bern let me out at my house, Franke, who was still distressed, asked me to return with her to Rowan Oak the next morning.

The night before at my house, I read *A Fable*, which was

very long. I was disappointed in most of the manuscript. Some of it I considered magnificent; other parts were badly organized. Bill had certainly made nothing easy for readers, and I thought it was often too obscure and lethargic. On the way to Oxford with Franke the second time I tried to think how I would express my feelings honestly about *A Fable*.

At Rowan Oak we found Bill asleep, this time on the couch in his study. His skin was yellowish and beneath his eyes were dark smudges. He had not undressed. Someone had laid a blanket over him, but it had fallen on the floor. Franke and I immediately left the room.

"This is awful," she said furiously. "Those people Mr. Faulkner said stayed out there in the cabin aren't tending to him. I'm going out there this minute and tell them they should be looking after him properly."

There were a couple of bottles lying by the sofa, one a whiskey bottle, the other containing some wine. Malcolm came into the room and Bill awakened when we began talking. With half-opened eyes, he looked at me. "Hello, fellow, hello, Malcolm. I'll be all right," and he dozed off again.

Malcolm and I went to the porch and were joined by Franke. "I could just kill them. I could just shoot every one of them. Excuse me, Malcolm, but I took the liberty of telling off those people. They should be ashamed of themselves neglecting him. I told them to get in this room and straighten up. I asked where the liquor came from, and they said that he had sent them for it. What a mess!"

Malcolm said he was giving Bill vitamin shots and raw eggs. Malcolm, Franke, and I conferred on the porch. Then we left for home again. But that wasn't the last of it. I decided that I had better go back to Oxford to see about him. I asked Major William Schultz of the medical department at the Base to take me to Oxford. Upon our arrival, we found things were deplorable.

When we entered the study, we saw that Bill apparently had fallen from the sofa and lay beside it. He was unwashed and no one had cleaned him. It was an ugly sight. His face looked even more mask-like than it had the day before and his skin had now become ashen. I turned to Major Schultz and asked him to go on the porch.

In the downstairs washroom, I wet cloths and made an effort to clean Bill. The telephone rang in the study. It did not seem to awaken him, and I answered it quietly. It was a woman, asking to speak to Mr. Faulkner. I replied that he wasn't well and couldn't come to the telephone. "Oh," she said hesitantly. "Just tell him Joan telephoned."

The phone had awakened Bill. "Who was it?" he asked, his voice faint.

"She said to tell you Joan called. That was all."

"God. Godamighty," he said, and went to sleep.

As I continued my inadequate ministrations, the phone rang again, a call from Hollywood. It was Howard Hawks's office, "for Mr. William Faulkner." I reported that Bill wasn't at home but that I would give him a message.

"Tell Mr. Faulkner that Mr. Hawks is planning to direct a picture in Egypt and wishes him to come along as writer on the script. Please have Mr. Faulkner call Mr. Hawks."

I wrote notes on paper I found in his workroom, giving Bill the two messages. By now Malcolm had come, and I asked him to be sure Bill received the messages. We went to the porch to talk, and Malcolm said he believed the best thing to do would be to take Bill to the sanitarium in Byhalia, where he had recuperated before and where he could receive medical and nursing care. I agreed, and Malcolm said he would make the arrangements.

In the study again, a great sense of sorrow came over me as I looked at Bill lying on the floor in a nearly comatose state. I looked, too, at the portrait above him on the wall. Miss Maud was so proud of it. I thought—and perhaps it was sentimental—how tragic the contrast of the two was. There, a young lad untouched by life, innocent, unscarred spiritually. And there, too, an aging man who had fame and money and many of our world's great honors, beset now by his own, and perhaps secret, horrors and despairs. I was so saddened by the anguish on his tragic face that I turned and left the room.

Jill was to be married in the summer of 1954, the wedding to take place at Oxford in St. Peter's Episcopal Church. The ceremony was to be followed by a reception in Estelle's rose garden. I wrote Bill to suggest that Bern might be engaged to take wedding and reception pictures, and Bill asked for us to drive over and discuss it.

Bern was and, I suppose, continues to be, an excellent dancer. Jill also loved to dance, so she and Bern hit it off immediately. At Rowan Oak in the small room to the rear of the entrance hall the two danced and danced to Jill's excellent collection of records. Estelle and I sat on the sidelines and watched, especially their expert tango.

Estelle finally told them to stop when she heard Bill enter the house. He joined us and asked me if it didn't seem strange that his little girl was getting married and leaving them. Jill protested that she'd never really leave them.

Her fiancé was Paul Summers. Estelle had told me that the young people were very much in love and that both she and Bill approved the match.

Bern and Bill went to the workroom to make plans for the wedding pictures. Bern had not seen Bill since the unfortunate meal at Rowan Oak and the day that followed. None of us, of course, mentioned that unpleasant time.

Jill's wedding was on a torrid summer day. I rode to Oxford with Bern, who was in high glee that he was to take pictures. We checked into the Alumni House at Ole Miss, where wedding guests were milling about the lobby after a pre-wedding luncheon.

Among the guests, I was happy to see Saxe Commins. He was Bill's special editor at Random House. His wife Dorothy was with him. Carvel Collins, the literary critic who was writing a biography of Bill, was the only Faulkner critic invited for the nuptials. I saw many other old acquaintances, and as soon as I stepped into the lobby, I began to have a very festive feeling.

Bern and I dressed for the wedding at the Alumni House and then went to Rowan Oak. Estelle was upstairs helping Jill into her wedding dress, and Bill was, I was told, in his workroom downstairs. Bern and I went in. Bill told Bern to take pictures as it suited him and suggested that he might like to look things over and line up a few shots. Then Bern left.

Bill wasn't as cool and calm as he would have liked me to believe. He put on his shirt. "I despise these shirts. I never liked stiff collars or things tight around my neck. I feel like I'm choking." He asked about my mother, and I asked about Miss Maud. Going to his typewriter table, he picked up a copy of *A Fable*, newly published, and handed it to me. "I've been saving this until you came over today." I thanked him, opened the book, and read the inscription: "To Ben: much love, much long time."

"I hope," he said, "you like it better now than when you read the manuscript. Saxe really worked hard with me on it. He tells me the critics don't like it much, some saying

it's 'muddied.' I still believe in it. I don't write for critics.
Never have. And it's too late for me to start trying to please
them. Help me with this fool tie." I adjusted the ascot and
attempted to loosen his collar somewhat.

Shelby Foote came into the room, and he and Bill made
small talk. Bill put on his Prince Albert coat. He looked
very handsome and fitted most admirably the role of
Father of the Bride. His hair was cut fairly short and his
moustache trimmed neatly. "I rented this outfit, in Memphis," he said. "Just like I rented that fancy dress get-up I
wore in Sweden."

Before Shelby left us, he commented on the *Fable* outline on the walls of the room. One of the waiters who had
been hired from the Peabody Hotel in Memphis came in,
dressed in a red coat, and said that Mrs. Faulkner and Miss
Jill were ready to come downstairs. They were starting
down the stairway. Estelle looked charming and Jill radiant
and lovely in her white wedding gown and veil. Bill looked
up at her as she descended toward him, and there was
great love in his eyes. He appeared to be content and
happy, beaming at his wife and cherished daughter. As
they reached the last step, one of the waiters brought
champagne on a tray.

"A toast together," Bill said, after kissing Jill and then
Estelle. "And you join us, Ben." I declined as graciously as
I could, and Estelle declared she didn't care for a drink,
but Bill insisted and she took one. (Later, we realized that
Estelle had been wise refusing the drink, for the one she
took under pressure led her to too many afterwards.) Bern
made several pictures of the bride, her mother, her father
glowingly toasting one another.

"It's time to go. Come with us to the car, Ben." I followed them. As Bill helped Estelle and Jill into the car,
another waiter came to ask him if there were any final

Jill Faulkner and her father

instructions to be given. Bill replied, "Be sure that the wine is cooled properly," and got in with Jill and Estelle.

In the church vestibule, an usher informed me that I was to be seated in the family pew. This touched me deeply.

Bill, Jill, and the bridegroom were as radiant a nuptial trio as I had ever seen. The small church was charmingly decorated with flowers and candles. Having given Jill to the bridegroom, Bill returned to the pew and joined us.

Afterwards, friends and relatives chatted outside the church, then returned to Rowan Oak for the reception. There was an air of geniality and happiness, and when the supply of champagne was exhausted, the waiters served white wine. Bill and Estelle continuously circulated among the guests. Bill came to Carvel Collins and me in a corner of the garden and asked us to try to restrain an inebriated guest, who was becoming obstreperous. Carvel said he would take care of it. Bill said he didn't wish anything ugly to mar the event and that too much drinking was inexcusable and very bad-mannered.

As the bride and bridegroom were pelted with rice while dashing to their automobile to leave for their honeymoon, I saw that Bill, for a moment caught off-guard, looked downcast. He and Estelle stood together, with wine-glasses in their hands, watching the automobile drive away from Rowan Oak.

It was in the next year, 1955, on one of those wintry days that turn suddenly to summer, when the cars drove up to Rowan Oak. Sitting on the steps beneath the white columns, and framed in the dark arch of Faulknerian green, was our host, William Faulkner.

But this is getting somewhat ahead. Before that, in October, a motion picture company had made headquarters in Greenville and, with Elia (Gadg) Kazan as its director, were

Carvel Collins, Ben Wasson, and Saxe Commins at Jill
Faulkner's wedding reception

making a film of Tennessee Williams's *Baby Doll*. The company was on location in the small Delta town of Benoit, twenty miles from Greenville, and most of the scenes were filmed at an old run-down mansion close to Benoit. Some of the people in the film, crew members, and camera assistants (but none of the four stars, who were working) wished to go to Oxford and meet William Faulkner. Among them were Jean Stein and Marguerite Lamkin. Both were working for Kazan, the latter coaching actors to speak a deep Southern dialect. Miss Stein, an exceptionally pretty young woman with dark hair and creamy magnolia skin, was said by the movie folks to be more than a close friend of Bill. On the phone to Bill I told him that several people in the crew wanted to come to Oxford. He asked me to gather the party and bring them on up.

Two cars, holding about ten people of the *Baby Doll* crew, headed for Oxford. At Rowan Oak Bill greeted us wearing a crisp white shirt open at the neck, cuffs turned back, and freshly starched khaki trousers. He looked the "Virginia gentleman." After a round of introductions, he ushered us into the house and to his own sitting room rather than to the parlor. He explained that Estelle's mother, Mrs. Oldham, was gravely ill and that Estelle was with her, she and her sister Dorothy keeping an around-the-clock vigil at the bedside.

"I can offer you just about everything," Bill told his guests, a charming twinkle in his eyes, his voice holding its usual soft inflection. "I make a real good martini." After the martinis were made and passed around, Molly Kazan, the director's wife, complimented him on the excellence of the martini. "Four to one is the secret," he told them. "Very, very dry—the best gin, of course."

Then she began to tell a story which apparently she had prepared in advance. "I've made a friend on the *Baby Doll*

Karl Malden and Carroll Baker in Benoit, Mississippi, during the filming of *Baby Doll*, about 1953

Elia Kazan, Tennessee Williams, and Ben Wasson, Greenville, 1952

set at Benoit, and he's getting to be a problem. His name is Boll Weevil. At least that's the only name I've heard him called."

"And he's a perfectly marvelous person," Jean Stein added.

Mrs. Kazan turned to me: "I presume he has another name?"

"If he has one, I don't know it," I said.

"Since he's an actor in the picture, I wonder if Gadg will list him in the acting credits as 'Boll Weevil,' which at least will puzzle audiences. He's a black farmhand on Charlie Boy Williams's plantation where Gadg discovered him when he came down here to make the picture. Yesterday, Boll Weevil came to me and told me, 'Miss Molly, I want to move up North and work for you and Mr. Gadg.' I protested that he probably wouldn't care for the frozen North, and so forth. But Boll Weevil was adamant. He has made up his mind. He said, 'I'm going to bring three dozen chickens with me. Us can put 'em in the deep freeze and eat 'em when us feels like it.' He was obviously sure I'd be dazzled by this offer—I was! But, Mr. Faulkner, what do you think I should do? Do you think Boll Weevil would be happy in Connecticut?"

Bill, now aglow with mock solemnity and gallantry for the seemingly troubled lady, rose to the proffered bait.

"Mrs. Kazan, I'd be happy to answer your question about Boll Weevil. I know his kind very well. If he's going to present you with three dozen chickens, you must take him North and take him at once. Because when the word gets out about those chickens, he's going to have to move somewhere. The next county might not be far enough away."

This was the only amusing point in an otherwise solemn, staid "drop in" with many serious questions being put to Bill about the race question and Bill fielding most of the interrogations very well.

Bill had been as pleasant and casual a host as anyone
could have wished. It was getting late and Mrs. Kazan said
we should be returning to Greenville. "Call us when you
come to New York again, Mr. Faulkner," and her invitation
was echoed by the others.

Miss Stein and I were the only ones in the group already
acquainted with Bill. Throughout the entire visit he had
been to a group of strangers courteous, dignified, simple,
and direct and altogether a true lord of the manor.

The weather in the Delta had become wretched and so cold
and damp that Kazan decided it would be more practical to
complete *Baby Doll* in a Brooklyn studio. So, following the
Christmas holidays, the company returned East with a
short schedule of shooting that remained. Soon after they
left Mississippi, I went to New York to be on hand for
completion of the film.

I knew that Bill was in the city because I had been
invited by Miss Stein the day before to come to her apartment on the East River for lunch. Bill, Shelby Foote, and
Dick Sylbert, the set designer for *Baby Doll*, were to be
there.

"Mr. Faulkner couldn't come," Miss Stein said when we
gathered at her apartment. But Miss Stein, Foote, Sylbert,
and I had a delightful lunch together. We reminisced about
Greenville and Benoit and some of the amusing, colorful
things that happened during the filming.

After lunch I strolled along Madison Avenue. As I was
about to pass the building in which the offices of Random
House were then situated, I suddenly decided that I would
like to see Bennett Cerf again. I had always been fond of
him, and our relationship during my years as an agent in
New York had been most cordial. On the spur of the moment I entered the building. I told the receptionist my
name, and she said that Bennett was out of town for several

days. As I was about to leave, she said, "Oh, Mr. Wasson, Mr. Faulkner is upstairs in Mr. Commins's office. Wouldn't you like for me to let them know you are here?"

I told her that I would like very much to see them if they weren't too busy. She rang Saxe's office, and Saxe told her to send me to them.

Saxe and Bill were intent over some typewritten pages. Saxe was extremely cordial. But Bill greeted me as he might have greeted an utter stranger. He was wholly aloof, and the few words he addressed to me were indifferent and spoken without warmth.

Saxe, no doubt feeling Bill's obvious estrangement from me, talked on and on about the pleasure he and his wife Dorothy had when they were in Mississippi for Jill's wedding. He attempted to draw Bill into the conversation, but Bill became even more withdrawn.

It was then I realized that nothing was going to thaw him out. Feeling the pain this brought me, I didn't know what to say. Suddenly, unable to stand his inexplicable antagonism, I got up from my chair and said that I should be leaving. Saxe, obviously embarrassed, took my elbow and walked to the door with me. I knew my face must have been red with embarrassment and hurt.

Saxe kept me at the door for a short while and talked politely about a number of things, but to this day I have no recollection of a word he said. Saxe's attempt to be kind to me only made me feel sicker at heart. I could not bear another minute for I knew that for some reason this was the end of a wonderful friendship that had survived through many years. I still do not know why Bill turned against me, and I never asked him. I never saw him again.

As I bade Saxe good-bye, sending greetings to Dorothy and to Bennett when he returned, I looked back to Bill sitting in the chair by Saxe's desk.

He said, his voice low, "Good-bye, Bud."

Ben and Meta during the filming of *The Reivers*, Carrollton, Mississippi, 1968

Ben Wasson with Leon Koury's clay sculpture of William Faulkner

Some Names in the Text

Bel Geddes, Norman. Stage designer for Max Reinhardt's *The Miracle Worker* and more than two hundred other theatrical presentations. Producer.

Brickell, Henry Herschel. Born in Mississippi. Newspaperman. Literary critic. Book columnist and literary editor, New York *Post*. Editor, ten annual volumes of O. Henry Award prize stories.

Carlisle, Helen Grace (pen name of Helen Grace Reid). Author, *See How They Run, Mothers Cry, The Wife*.

Cobb, Elizabeth. Biographer, of her father Irvin S. Cobb in *My Wayward Parent*.

Cobb, Irvin S. Newspaperman. Humorist. Author, stories about Judge Priest, travel books. Scriptwriter. Actor.

Connelly, Marc[us Cook]. Playwright, with George S. Kaufman *Dulcy* and *To the Ladies!* and *Be Yourself, The Wisdom Tooth, The Green Pastures* (Pulitzer Prize). Scriptwriter.

Crouse, Russel. Author, *Mr. Currier and Mr. Ives, It Seems Like Yesterday*. Librettist for musical comedies. Playwright, with Howard Lindsay the stage version of Clarence Day's *Life with Father, State of the Nation* (Pulitzer Prize). Producer with Lindsay *Arsenic and Old Lace*.

Crump, Owen. Painter. Playwright, *Southern Exposure*. Scriptwriter.

Devine, James Eric. Author and editor of books on yachting.

Emerson, John. Actor. Producer. Author (with wife, Anita Loos), *Breaking into the Movies* and *The Whole Town's Talking*.

Ford, Corey. Humorist, *Salt Water Taffy, Coconut Oil, The Office Party*. Parodist under the pen name of "John Riddell," *In the Worst Possible Taste*.

Guinzburg, Harold K. Publisher, Viking Press, founder and director of The Literary Guild.

Hamilton, Marise. The Metropolitan Opera House box mentioned in the text was that of her uncle J. Pierpont Morgan.

Hawkins, Arthur. Designer. Painter. Art director. Author.
Hughes, Richard Arthur Warren. Poet. Author, *A High Wind in Jamaica*, *In Hazard*.
Johnson, Nunnally. Story writer. Scriptwriter. Film producer.
Loos, Anita. Scriptwriter. Author, *Gentlemen Prefer Blondes*, *A Girl Like I*, *Breaking into the Movies* (with husband, John Emerson).
Lovett, Robert. Banker.
O'Neil, George. Poet. Playwright, *American Dream*, *Mother Lode* in collaboration with Dan Totheroh.
Parker, Dorothy. Poet, *Enough Rope*, *Collected Poems: Not So Deep as a Well*. Story writer, *Here Lies: The Collected Stories*. Playwright. Drama critic. Book reviewer.
Percy, William Alexander. Lawyer. Poet, *Sappho in Levkas and Other Poems*, *In April Once*, *Enzio's Kingdom and Other Poems*. Autobiographer, *Lanterns on the Levee*.
King, Muriel. Fashion designer.
Saalburg, Allen. Painter. Illustrator. Printmaker.
Saxon, Lyle. Writer, *Fabulous New Orleans*, *Old Louisiana*, *Children of Strangers*.
Silver, James. Professor of History, University of Mississippi, later University of Notre Dame and University of South Florida. Author, *Edmond Pendleton Gaines: Frontier General*, *Mississippi: The Closed Society*.
Spencer, Elizabeth. Novelist, *Fire in the Morning*, *This Crooked Way*, *The Voice at the Back Door*, *The Light in the Piazza*. Story writer, *Ship Island and Other Stories*.
Stone, Jim. Phil Stone's brother.
Sullivan, Frank. Humorist, *Life and Times of Martha Hepplethwaite*, *The Adventures of an Oaf*, *A Pearl in Every Oyster*.
Totheroh, Dan W. Playwright, *Wild Birds*, *The Last Dragon*, *Distant Drums*, *Mother Lode* in collaboration with George O'Neill. Novelist, *Wild Orchard*, *Deep Valley*.
Van Vechten, Carl. Critic. Author, *In the Garret*, *Interpreters*, *The Blind Bow-Boy*. Editor, *Selected Works of Gertrude Stein*. Photographer.

Index